May

THE WAY OUT OF THE WILDERNESS

Learn How Bible Heroes with Feet of Clay Are Models for Your Recovery

---

EARL R. HENSLIN, Psy.D.

THOMAS NELSON
Nashville

Published in Nashville, Tennessee, by Thomas Nelson, Inc., and
distributed in Canada by Lawson Falle, Ltd., Cambridge, Ontario.

Scripture quotations are from The Holy Bible: NEW INTERNATIONAL
VERSION. Copyright © 1978 by the New York International Bible
Society. Used by permission of Zondervan Bible Publishers.

The names of persons and certain details of case histories described
in this book have been changed to protect the author's clients. In
certain cases, composite case histories have been constructed from
actual cases.

Library of Congress Cataloging-in-Publication Data

Henslin, Earl R.
    The way out of the wilderness : learn how Bible heroes with feet
of clay are models for your recovery / Earl R. Henslin.
        p.   cm.
    Includes bibliographical references.
    ISBN 0-8407-7662-4
    1. Adult children of dysfunctional families—Religious life.
2. Codependents—Religious life. 3. Shame—Religious aspects-
-Christianity. 4. Problem families—Biblical teaching. 5. Family-
-Religious life. I. Title.
BV4596.A274H46   1991
248.8'6—dc20   91–30431
                                                    CIP

Printed in the United States of America

1 2 3 4 5 6 7 — 96 95 94 93 92 91

FOREWORD

Here at last is a well-trained psychologist who understands family dynamics and dysfunction from a sound theological basis and from personal experience. He sees the source of disease and recovery from a biblical perspective, has faced his codependence, and is in recovery from his own parental-family of origin issues. Earl Henslin, through this extraordinary book, helps Christians see the source of the bewildering emotional pain and frustration in our lives and particularly in our close relationships.

He has described with great clarity how we as individuals and as committed Christians have problems stemming from the way we were raised even by well-meaning parents. Our parents may even have been fine Christians, but did not understand how they were setting us up to be filled with exaggerated feelings of shame and inadequacy (as well as oversized fear, resentment, anger, sadness, emotional pain and loneliness). Since both *their* parents and they were committed to Jesus Christ, these Christians have often felt guilty about having these painful feelings, as if they indicated a lack of faith or commitment.

We come to see in these pages that even if we deny the feelings and "numb" them, the feelings continue to manifest themselves in our close relationships with people, God, and ourselves, causing us to unconsciously neglect, abandon, and otherwise abuse our mates and children. Dr. Henslin shows how we get into compulsive religious work to try to kill the pain of our secret feelings of not being enough.

Without blaming or accusing, Earl shows us how this pain comes about, how it brings misery and loneliness in families, and how God has provided a way of recovery that can bring serenity and new life to Christians and non-Christians alike.

One of the things that makes this book extremely valuable to the Christian community is that Earl illustrates with great insight some of the problems of codependence and family dysfunction from the lives of outstanding biblical characters like David, Solomon, and even Jesus. And as he moves on to talk about recovery for Christians, he is able to discuss the necessary therapeutic process clearly, while pointing us directly to the person of Jesus Christ as the ultimate source of the power for recovery and the healing itself. There is also specific information on how and where to get help.

I predict this book will help thousands of Christians who have not been able to see and understand the pain and frustration in their lives, family relationships, and these less than satisfactory Christian journeys. I hope every adult Christian who is having baffling conflict with family members, doubt about his or her adequacy in personal or vocational areas, or feeling dry and distant about his or her relationship to God will read this book.

J. Keith Miller
Austin, Texas

Acknowledgments

Many people have supported me and have played a role in the development of this book. The following are just a few of the people God has placed in my life to help support me and to whom I do my best to give support. This list may seem lengthy, yet it reveals the depth of the support that enables me to live each day and accomplish the work I do.

First and foremost, I thank my wife, Karen. She has been with me and beside me through my journey of recovery for nearly eighteen years. Her willingness to support me in this project has been a gift from God. I also want to thank Ben, Rachel, Amy, and Jill for their support and encouragement. Children are a gift from God, and I hope I can continue to grow in my efforts to encourage them in pursuing the gifts with which God has blessed them.

I want to thank my dad and mom for their willingness to share about our family. I appreciate their willingness to talk about and work through the difficult issues. I also thank Tom, Bruce, and Sandra for their support and for forgiving me for the craziness that only a brother could bring to their lives.

I thank Greataunt Lenora, now ninety-five years old, who has faithfully modeled God's grace and love for me. I thank her for praying for me daily since I was fourteen years old. Her support and encouragement have meant so much to me. I also thank Karen's grandmother, Grandma Englehardt, who is a constant model of the meaning and purpose of life, even when it is lived through chronic pain.

Fred and Virginia Palke, Karen's parents, are also special to me. I appreciate the way they have modeled good boundaries and have expressed their warmth and support of our family. I also thank my brothers- and sisters-in-law, Sue and Ed Evenson and Tom and Kathy Palke for their unfailing caring and support.

I thank Bill Henslin, now eighty-five years old, who God has used to touch my heart in ways that only he could have done. I share in his sadness that his brother Elmer is no longer here to share the joy of completing this project. Yet I am thankful that he is rejoicing with us in heaven. I also thank my Uncle Norman who has consistently expressed his interest and support of me since I was a little boy.

I want to thank my friends Will Hawkins, Vance and Beth Shepperson, Sam and Judy Doolittle, Steve and Donalyn Elliott, Lynn and Lucy Oliver, Midge Finley, Keith Miller, and Steve and Linda Youngerberg, who have faithfully supported and encouraged me over the years. I also thank my friend and office manager, Marguerite Miller, for her faithfulness and encouragement in my practice and in the development of this book.

I thank Ron and Sue Arnold for helping me meet Ron Haynes of Thomas Nelson Publishers. A special thanks to Amanda and Stephen Sorenson, whose writing and editorial support during this project have made it possible for this message of recovery to be heard.

I am blessed in having known Eve D. who was willing to share the wisdom and insight she gained through more than twenty-five years of recovery in A.A. She took me to my first A.A. meeting and was the first person God used to help me feel the meaning of love and acceptance. I thank Bob and Pauline B., whose recovery, friendship, and invitation to participate in Overcomers Outreach have been a blessing. I also thank the following men who have been special mentors to me: Dr. David Klimek, John Wera, Jim Nagel, Dr. Ben Cooley, Dr. Stuart Cooke, Jerry Hurdlik, Dr. Keith Edwards, and Dr. Bill Hunter.

I offer a special thanks for the friendship and ministry of Chuck Swindoll. Sitting under his teaching has been one of the greatest experiences of my life. His faithful exposition of Scripture has been the inspiration behind the biblical portion of this book. Pastors Jim Dinsmore, Matt Hannon, Dave Carder, John Columbe, Buck Buchanan, and Gary Richmond have also provided special support and encouragement to me.

Finally, I thank all the patients who have been willing to share their recovery with me and have been willing to do whatever it takes to continue in recovery. I thank all the people I know in twelve-step programs. Their lives are a testimony of God's healing!

I dedicate this book to my wife, Karen. Her love, support, encouragement, and commitment to me, our marriage, and our children mean everything to me.

PREFACE

For more than a decade I have had the privilege of learning through my pastor's frank, direct, and honest exposition of Scripture. One Sunday, as he spoke on David's life, it suddenly struck me that David's family suffered great emotional pain. As I thought about the story of David, Amnon, Tamar, Absalom, and Solomon, I felt the feelings that were familiar when I was a little boy—feelings that every individual, couple, and family brings into my office.

Because I am a therapist that discovery fascinated me and prompted me to study the families of the Bible in greater depth. My study has revealed not one family in the Bible that was free from some painful struggle or hurt—or as we would say today, some dysfunction. It was as if a giant light had suddenly flashed on, allowing me to feel a bit more of God's grace. Suddenly God became more real to me. I realized that He does not want us to live superficially with the pretense that our lives are okay.

Centuries of family history recorded in the Bible reveal that biblical families faced the same issues families face today. Just as many families do today, hurting, biblical families tended to deny their problems and their pain. They pretended to live as if everything was okay, but their lives weren't okay. Story after story reveals alcoholism, marriages that lacked intimacy, sexual addiction and abuse, codependency, and even murder!

Through my pastor's teaching, I realized that God's grace goes beyond perfection. He wants to meet us in our everyday struggles—where we live spiritually, emotionally, and relationally. The sad truth is, in our perfectionistic and at times self-righteous Christian community, we often value outward appearances more than inner feelings. We often are insensitive to what is really happening in the life of the person sitting next to us. We tend to expect perfection and reject those who have problems. In fact David, the man after God's own heart, most likely would not be welcome in our churches and definitely would not make it on a church staff!

Through my study of biblical families, the ministry of my pastor, and the caring challenges of several mentors, I realized that if my marriage and my children were to have a chance to reach their potential, the cycle of dysfunction in our lives needed to be broken. I, too, needed to admit that I was a hurting person who needed healing. I needed to begin a journey of recovery.

My years of work as a therapist had made me a participant in the lives of many struggling families. I had seen God bring about deep changes when family members finally faced the hurt they had lived with since childhood. However, I never realized the level at which God could work in my life until I attended my first Alcoholics Anonymous meeting about twenty years ago. I wasn't an alcoholic, but in A.A. I discovered that God could accomplish the same healing of hurts in my life that I had seen Him accomplish in the lives of recovering alcoholics and their families.

Encouraged by what I had seen, I began my own recovery. For four years, Ollie Backus, Ph.D., led me on a journey to discover the hurting child deep within me. I also participated in a twelve-step recovery group where others who were honestly facing their own struggles accepted me and my inadequacies. I was overwhelmed by their unconditional love, a love without shame, that I had rarely experienced even in the Christian community. For the first time in my life, I had the freedom to discover and deal with my deepest secrets and pain. I had begun a journey toward healing: a journey that would help me, my wife, and my children face our hurts and break the patterns of dysfunction that occurred when we tried to live as if everything was okay.

In recent years, I have spoken to a number of church groups, sharing my professional and personal experiences with family dysfunction and recovery. When I speak, I often retell the stories of dysfunctional biblical families. These stories are received with tears of relief. Afterward, Christians who have grown up with the hidden pain of alcoholism, codependency, incest, and other symptoms of dysfunction come up to talk with me. They express tremendous relief that they aren't alone in their pain, that even some of the most "spiritual" families in Scripture faced similar issues.

I believe the Christian community today needs to accept the reality of family dysfunction and become a part of the healing process. For too long, we have shot our wounded with shame rather than offering the healing arms of Christ's grace and understanding. The time to pretend that Christians are perfect is over. It needs to be okay for Christians to struggle through problems and deep hurts in order to heal.

Thankfully this is beginning to happen. When I began my recovery twenty years ago, A.A. and the way in which God used the twelve steps to help people, was completely disconnected from the Christian community. But today increasing numbers of churches are starting twelve-step support-group ministries that provide a healing community for fellow strugglers. When we allow God to heal the hurting child within us through such a community, our marriages have a greater chance to survive. Our children have a better opportunity to face life with less hurt, and they have greater ability to deal with the hurt they do have.

Today we have an opportunity to break the painful cycles of dysfunction under which so many biblical families suffered. A client once said to me, "Maybe Christ has not returned because He does not want to come back to a dysfunctional bride!" Whether his statement is true or not, he makes a valid point. We have the opportunity to help Christ's church become the healing, loving community He intends it to be. It is time for Christ's bride to turn away from dysfunction and accept the healing He offers.

CONTENTS

PART III
Roadmap for Recovery

PART I

Spiritually Minded, Emotionally Inept

Chapter 1

David: A Golden Hero
With Feet of Clay

King David is probably one of the best-loved people in the Bible. From the time we are very young, Sunday school teachers and parents tell us stories of David's exciting adventures as a young shepherd, his amazing exploits as a warrior, his adrenaline-pumping escapes from the wrath of King Saul, and his ascent as king of Judah and Israel. Once we mature beyond our youthful, adventure-story approach to Scripture, David again captivates our hearts through his psalms. Their painfully—and at times, laboriously—honest expression of his innermost thoughts often touch a deep chord within us. It's no exaggeration to say that David ranks as the golden hero of Scripture.

The reputation is well deserved. As a young shepherd alone in the wilderness, David rescued lambs from the mouths of bears and lions. When the angry beasts turned on him, David fearlessly grabbed them with his hands and killed them (see 1 Sam. 17:34–36). With just one stone thrown from his sling, the youthful David felled Goliath, the mighty Philistine giant (see 1 Sam. 17:49–50). Honored with a high rank in Saul's army, David lived up to and surpassed King Saul's expectations (see 1 Sam. 18:5).

Let's face it. David had just about everything going for him. Even King Saul's servants admired him. One of them described David as one "who knows how to play the harp. He is a brave man and a warrior. He speaks well and is a fine-looking man. And the Lord is with him" (1 Sam. 16:18). What more could anyone ask for? In addition to being good looking and having the finely tuned physique of a warrior, David was a talented musician and a dynamic speaker. Even disgruntled King Saul liked him (see 1 Sam. 16:21)!

Most significant, God had chosen David to be king of Israel. While David was still a youth, Samuel, Israel's high priest, went to the house of Jesse to anoint God's chosen king. As was customary Samuel first considered Jesse's oldest son, Eliab, who looked like a great prospect. But God told Samuel that Eliab wasn't the one, nor were six of his younger brothers. As a last resort, David, the youngest son and therefore the most unlikely candidate, was called in from the pastures where he tended sheep. When David arrived, the Lord told Samuel to anoint him. So in the presence of his older brothers, David was anointed as Israel's future king, and God's power came upon him (see 1 Sam. 16:12–13).

After he was anointed, David continued in King Saul's service. The people loved him. Saul's officers loved him. Jonathan, Saul's son, became David's best friend. Saul even gave David one of his daughters in marriage. In time, however, Saul became jealous of David and tried to kill him. Despite Saul's numerous attempts on his life, David remained Saul's faithful servant. On two occasions David even turned away from the opportunity to kill Saul, waiting instead for the Lord to accomplish His promises.

An Unsurpassed Devotion to God

David's eagerness to maintain righteousness and intimacy with God is perhaps this Bible hero's greatest characteristic. In fact, evidence of David's intimate relationship with God exists throughout his life. In some of David's psalms we see the euphoria of success as he rejoices in what God has done. In some we see his pain as he pours out his anguish to God. In others we see vibrant proclamations of God's faithfulness to His people. In the historical record of David's life (see 1 and 2 Sam. and 1 Kings) we see that David repeatedly asked God where he should go, what he should do, and whether or not he should go into battle. Furthermore, when David stumbled and indulged in sin, he willingly recognized his sin and sought reconciliation with God.

God, who judges the heart, was clearly pleased with David's spiritual condition. In 1 Kings 11:4 we read, "As Solomon grew old, his wives turned his heart after other gods, and his heart was not fully devoted to the LORD his God, *as the heart of David his father had been*" (italics added). Years later, the prophet Ahijah gave Jeroboam the following message from God: "I tore the kingdom away from the house of David and gave it to you, *but you have not been like my servant David, who kept my commands and followed me with all his heart*" (1 Kings 14:8, italics added). God repeatedly confirms His pleasure in the faithfulness of David's heart in other portions of Scripture as well (see also 1 Kings 11:6 and 15:3).

No doubt about it, David had a magnificent record. However, there was one "giant" that David never defeated. Although he experienced great triumph, David failed miserably in one area of life: his relationships with his family.

Apparently David never learned how to deal with emotion in family relationships. The intimacy, understanding, and openness of heart that David experienced with God were lacking in his relationships with his children. In fact, there was a great deal of emotional pain—yes, dysfunction—in David's family. The lack of emotional intimacy and its dire consequences are evident in David's relationships with his children Amnon, Tamar, and Absalom (see 2 Sam. 13–18:33).

David's Secret Sin

To understand the relational dynamics between David and his children, we need to consider a series of events that

occurred when Amnon, Tamar, and Absalom were teenagers. The story begins in 2 Samuel 11:1–5:

> *In the spring, at the time when kings go off to war, David*
> *sent Joab out with the king's men and the whole Israel-*
> *ite army. They destroyed the Ammonites and besieged*
> *Rabbah. But David remained in Jerusalem.*
>
> *One evening David got up from his bed and walked*
> *around on the roof of the palace. From the roof he saw a*
> *woman bathing. The woman was very beautiful, and*
> *David sent someone to find out about her. The man said,*
> *"Isn't this Bathsheba, the daughter of Eliam and the*
> *wife of Uriah the Hittite?" Then David sent messengers*
> *to get her. She came to him, and he slept with her. (She*
> *had purified herself from her uncleanness.) Then she*
> *went back home. The woman conceived and sent word*
> *to David, saying, "I am pregnant."*

Although spring was the time of year when kings went
off to war, David chose to stay at home. We don't know why
he made this decision, but evidently it was a poor one.
David wasn't where he belonged. He was restless and lonely.
The restlessness became boredom and idleness—fertile
ground for the seeds of sin.

In his restlessness, David saw Bathsheba and wanted
her. He knew that she was married to one of his soldiers,
but he slept with her anyway. Afterward he sent her home.
David probably thought that was the end of it, but Bathsheba had become pregnant. Suddenly David had an undeniable problem that he had to resolve. Lacking the courage
to face up to what he had done, he devised a plan to cover
up his sin. Unfortunately, the situation became more com-
plicated than he had intended.

Plan A was to have Uriah, Bathsheba's husband, go
home so he could sleep with Bathsheba (see 2 Sam. 11:6–
8). The plan was simple: David would send for Uriah and
they would talk about the war. David would send Uriah
home where he would sleep with his wife. Uriah would go
back to war, Bathsheba would have the baby, and no one
would be the wiser. The plan would have worked, except

Uriah was a more loyal soldier than David realized. Uriah modeled himself after David, a noble warrior, and he refused himself the comfort of sleeping with his wife while the rest of the army was at war (see 2 Sam. 11:9–11)!

Next, David tried Plan B, a more desperate attempt to manipulate Uriah into covering up David's sin. This plan was to get Uriah drunk so that he would go home and sleep with his wife. As intended, Uriah got drunk, but David's plan failed when again Uriah refused to go home (see 2 Sam. 11:12–13).

Plan C was David's ultimate tactic. He sent Uriah back to the front lines with sealed orders that the loyal soldier was to die in battle. The plan worked. After Bathsheba mourned her husband's death, she became David's wife and gave birth to a son (see 2 Sam. 11:14–27).

Sin Plants the Seeds of Dysfunction

Perhaps David thought the situation was behind him and life could go on as before. But that was not to be. According to Scripture, this is the one time in David's life when God was greatly displeased with David's actions (see 2 Sam. 11:27). God was not about to let David, His faithful servant, live as if nothing had happened. Second Samuel 12:1–13 explains the process God used, through His prophet Nathan, to break through David's denial and cause him to face his sin.

When confronted with what he had done, David immediately confessed his sin. Nathan responded, "The LORD has taken away your sin. You are not going to die" (2 Sam. 12:13). David's relationship with God was restored, but his actions had grave consequences.

The first consequence of David's sin was that the son Bathsheba gave birth to became ill and died. The child's illness was devastating to David:

David pleaded with God for the child. He fasted and went into his house and spent the nights lying on the ground. The elders of his household stood beside him to get him

*up from the ground, but he refused, and he would not eat
any food with them.*

*On the seventh day the child died. David's servants
were afraid to tell him that the child was dead, for they
thought, "While the child was still living, we spoke to
David but he would not listen to us. How can we tell him
the child is dead? He may do something desperate."
(2 Sam. 12:16–18)*

Do you feel the intensity of David's emotion? The servants
were at a total loss to know what to do. We don't know why,
but they were afraid to approach him. Perhaps they were
afraid that he might do something drastic. After all, the previous king had been known to throw spears when he was
angry or depressed! But David's next actions confused
them even more.

When he learned that the child had died, David rose,
cleaned himself up, ate a meal, and went on with life. From
that point on, he lived as if nothing had happened. This was
more than the servants could handle!

*His servants asked him, "Why are you acting this way?
While the child was alive, you fasted and wept, but now
that the child is dead, you get up and eat!"*

*He answered, "While the child was still alive, I fasted
and wept. I thought, 'Who knows? The Lord may be gra-
cious to me and let the child live.' But now that he is
dead, why should I fast?" (2 Sam. 12:21–23)*

David's response reveals his motivation for fasting and
weeping: He wanted God to let the child live. After the child
died David did not allow himself to grieve the loss. In fact,
his feelings of grief did not surface until much later when he
began to grieve the loss of his older sons.

The second consequence of David's affair with Bathsheba and the subsequent death of their son was the emotional effect those events had on other family members,
particularly Amnon, Tamar, and Absalom. Imagine what it
was like for them to learn that their father had had an affair,
that he had arranged the death of their stepmother's hus-

band, and that their baby brother had died because of it. Imagine the emotional turmoil of the household—where even the servants didn't know what to do and were afraid to talk to David! Those teenagers had to bury many feelings in response to their father's actions because there was no way to talk about them within the family.

Unfortunately, Scripture gives no evidence that David dealt with the situation in relationship to his teenage children. Although he dealt with the situation in the context of his relationship with God, there is no evidence that the embarrassment of the affair and the pain of losing the child were ever dealt with on an emotional level within the family. Thus the affair with Bathsheba was merely the beginning. The family tragedies that followed were the consequences of this sin and the feelings associated with it that were never discussed or resolved.

Dysfunction Tends to Repeat Itself In Subsequent Generations

Family dysfunction often begins with an inability to handle emotions and tends to become more extreme as time passes. David's family was no exception. Second Samuel 13:1—19:3 tells the story of the dysfunction that appeared in the next generation of David's family.

> *In the course of time, Amnon son of David fell in love with Tamar, the beautiful sister of Absalom son of David.*
> *Amnon became frustrated to the point of illness on account of his sister Tamar, for she was a virgin, and it seemed impossible for him to do anything to her. (2 Sam. 13:1–2)*

Amnon, David's oldest son, faced an uncomfortable situation: He was desperately in love with Tamar, his younger half-sister. He was caught between his desire for her as a woman and the fact that she was his half-sister, which made an intimate relationship with her unthinkable. As a result, Amnon became physically ill. Apparently he was sick for some time because his friend Jonadab asked, "Why do you, the king's son, look so haggard morning after morning? Won't you tell me?" (2 Sam. 13:4)

Amnon told his troubles to Jonadab and, in the same way that David had planned to manipulate circumstances so that his adultery with Bathsheba would be covered up, the young men planned to manipulate David into sending Tamar to Amnon. "Amnon lay down and pretended to be ill. When the king came to see him, Amnon said to him, 'I would like my sister Tamar to come and make some special bread in my sight, so I may eat from her hand'" (2 Sam. 13:6). The plan worked. None the wiser, David sent Tamar to Amnon's house, where she prepared the food Amnon had requested.

When the food was prepared, Amnon sent everyone out of his house and asked Tamar to feed it to him in his bedroom. Second Samuel 13:11–18 reveals the emotional drama that ensued:

> But when she took it to him to eat, he grabbed her and said, "Come to bed with me, my sister."
>
> "Don't, my brother!" she said to him. "Don't force me. Such a thing should not be done in Israel! Don't do this wicked thing. What about me? Where could I get rid of my disgrace? And what about you? You would be like one of the wicked fools in Israel. Please speak to the king; he will not keep me from being married to you." But he refused to listen to her, and since he was stronger than she, he raped her.
>
> Then Amnon hated her with intense hatred. In fact, he hated her more than he had loved her. Amnon said to her, "Get up and get out!"
>
> "No!" she said to him. "Sending me away would be a greater wrong than what you have already done to me."
>
> But he refused to listen to her. He called his personal servant and said, "Get this woman out of here and bolt the door after her." So his servant put her out and bolted the door after her.

Throughout the ordeal Amnon refused to listen to Tamar's pleas. Afterward he was so ashamed of his incestuous act that he selfishly placed all of the shame on Tamar. His misguided love turned to violent hatred as he threw her out of his home.

The impact on Tamar was devastating. As the door to Amnon's house bolted shut behind her, she lost every bit of dignity and respect befitting a king's daughter. As a symbol of her loss, she tore her richly ornamented robe, a robe that was worn only by virgin daughters of the king. She put ashes on her head as a symbol of her grief and humiliation and went away, crying aloud as she went (see 2 Sam. 13:18–19).

On her way, she encountered her brother Absalom, who no doubt was shocked by her appearance. Suspiciously he asked, "Has that Amnon, your brother, been with you?" Perhaps with that question, Tamar felt a whisper of hope—someone would right the wrong that had been done to her. If so, her hope was soon crushed, for Absalom, in his inadequacy, quickly shamed her into silence with the words, "Be quiet now, my sister; he is your brother. Don't take this thing to heart" (2 Sam. 13:20). In effect he said, "Don't take this seriously, Tamar. This is a family matter that we have to handle with discretion, so please keep your composure."

Absalom's response to Tamar's pain is characteristic of dysfunctional families. Pain (like many other emotions) is avoided or denied, but never faced. For example, Absalom must have noticed something about Amnon—something that he would not or could not discuss—that led him to suspect the truth. When Tamar told him the truth, he had a perfect opportunity to embrace her and comfort her. Instead, he followed the family pattern of denial and clamped a tight lid on her pain, expecting her to keep it to herself.

What about their father? Unfortunately, David was no more adept at handling the situation than his children. The law required that the perpetrator of such a crime be stoned, or at least exiled. Yet Scripture indicates that David was furious (see 2 Sam. 13:21) but did nothing to punish Amnon and nothing to comfort Tamar. He reacted but then remained strangely silent and passive, offering no resolution to the crisis. From all appearances, it seemed nothing had happened.

Unresolved Family Pain Goes Underground

Appearances can be deceiving, however. Although Amnon's rape of Tamar created few ripples on the surface of palace life, an unbridled storm raged beneath the surface. David was furious. Shamed by Amnon's rape, Absalom's admonition, and David's inaction, Tamar lived in desolation. Amnon, denying his role, hated Tamar. Absalom so hated Amnon that he would not even speak to him. As in most dysfunctional families, these feelings did not lessen as time passed. In fact, they grew stronger.

After two years of strong, emotional reaction to the situation without any resolution of the real problem, Absalom could take no more. Perhaps he was frustrated by David's lack of initiative in confronting Amnon and reconciling the problem. Perhaps, because Absalom had brought his beloved sister into his home and therefore lived in close proximity to her pain, the burden of her desolation and shame became more than he could bear. Perhaps he simply could no longer hide his silent hatred for Amnon. Whatever the reason, Absalom moved to end the stalemate.

First he approached David and invited him, his officials, and the rest of the family to his home to celebrate the sheep-shearing season. David refused, saying that having the whole family together in one place would be too much of a burden for Absalom. Although Absalom urged him, David still refused. David did, however, give his blessing for the gathering. Absalom then asked if Amnon could join the festivities. The king questioned this request, but gave in when Absalom repeated it (see 2 Sam. 13:23–27).

Although Absalom did not directly say that he wanted to get the family together in order to deal with Amnon's actions, that was his intent (see 2 Sam. 13:32). David certainly knew that Absalom had strong feelings about what Amnon had done to Tamar; it was no secret in the palace. Yet direct communication is often difficult in dysfunctional families, so family members often try to achieve change through indirect means. When indirect means fail to produce change, a crisis often occurs. Thus the opportunity

Absalom presented may have been David's last chance to bring about healing in his family relationships.

With lamentable consistency, David again avoided the issue. Perhaps his affair with Bathsheba, the death of Uriah, and the loss of his infant son were more than David could face with his adult children, who were now living out his sin. Fed up with David's lack of response, Absalom took on his father's role and dealt with the situation himself. When Amnon arrived at Absalom's home,

> *Absalom ordered his men, "Listen! When Amnon is in high spirits from drinking wine and I say to you, 'Strike Amnon down,' then kill him. Don't be afraid. Have not I given you this order? Be strong and brave." So Absalom's men did to Amnon what Absalom had ordered. Then all the king's sons got up, mounted their mules and fled. (2 Sam. 13:28–29)*

David's oldest son was killed by Absalom in an attempt to bring the unresolved family secret to the surface. The result of the crisis? David was deeply grieved and Absalom went into hiding, but the original problem remained unchanged. The only real change was an increase in the family's pain through the loss of Amnon and a deepening rift between David and Absalom.

Absalom Escalates the Crisis

Most of us remember Absalom as the rebellious son who tried to wrest the kingdom from King David. Absalom was responsible for rebellious acts that clearly showed his inability to handle anger. Yet it is also evident that the root of Absalom's anger was inextricably linked to Tamar's hurt and David's lack of appropriate response to it. The sad truth of dysfunctional families is that family members are unwilling to admit their proper responsibilities for what happens in the family. As a result, one family member often acts out the pain that has not been faced by the rest of the family. One person becomes the rebellious scapegoat and in David's family, it was Absalom.

Fearing David's response to Amnon's death, Absalom went into hiding. Three years passed before David allowed him to return to Jerusalem. Even then, David refused to let Absalom see him (see 2 Sam. 14:23–24). Instead of allowing Absalom to seek forgiveness and work toward reconciliation, David added to Absalom's bitterness, anger, and shame. Although years had passed since Amnon raped Tamar, Absalom (as well as the rest of the family) still lived with the pain of that incident. In fact Absalom named his only daughter "Tamar," which indicates deep feeling for his wounded sister.

For two years Absalom lived in Jerusalem and waited for an opportunity to see David. Finally Absalom asked Joab to come to him so that Joab, who had access to David, could ask David to meet with Absalom. On two different occasions, Joab stoutly refused to see Absalom (see 2 Sam. 14:29). By this time, seven years after Amnon raped Tamar, Absalom's anger had again reached the boiling point, so he precipitated another crisis.

> Then he said to his servants, "Look, Joab's field is next to mine, and he has barley there. Go and set it on fire." So Absalom's servants set the field on fire.
>
> Then Joab did go to Absalom's house and he said to him, "Why have your servants set my field on fire?"
>
> Absalom said to Joab, "Look, I sent word to you and said, 'Come here so I can send you to the king to ask, "Why have I come from Geshur? It would be better for me if I were still there!"' Now then, I want to see the king's face, and if I am guilty of anything, let him put me to death."
>
> So Joab went to the king and told him this. Then the king summoned Absalom, and he came in and bowed down with his face to the ground before the king. And the king kissed Absalom. (2 Sam. 14:30–33)

Absalom certainly knew how to get attention! He so desperately wanted resolution in his relationship with his father, he was willing to die rather than continue living in isolation. He needed to be heard and know where he stood with his father, which is important for any child to know. So, at Absalom's initiation, David and Absalom faced each other. David kissed Absalom, indicating superficial affection for him, but no real change took place in their relationship.[1]

Although David and Absalom's meeting was a good step in the right direction, it did not bring about the healing needed. David's heart appears to have softened toward Absalom; however, Absalom's actions after this meeting suggest that David was still unwilling to deal with the real pain in his family. Absalom proceeded to inform Israel that David would not hear their needs or complaints, which is a direct reflection of Absalom's assessment of his family life. Soon the nation of Israel supported Absalom in a revolt against David (see 2 Sam. 15:1–23).

The family problem that David failed to deal with when Amnon raped Tamar had become an unbelievable crisis. Tamar lived in desolation; Amnon was murdered; Absalom was exiled. Eventually the whole nation of Israel became involved in a bitter war and Absalom met a violent, shameful death (see 2 Sam. 18:14–15).

Only after Absalom's death do we begin to see how much David really loved Absalom. David was greatly shaken. He grieved openly, saying, "O my son Absalom! My son, my son Absalom! If only I had died instead of you—O Absalom, my son, my son!" (2 Sam. 18:33). In the depths of his grieving, David must have reflected on the whole history of pain in his family—his affair with Bathsheba, the murder of Uriah, the death of his infant son, Amnon's rape of Tamar, Amnon's death at his brother's hand, and finally, Absalom's death.

What an incredible loss! David, the most powerful man in Israel, was absolutely crushed by Absalom's death. The burden of his family's pain—much of it carried on Absalom's shoulders—weighed heavily upon him. In fact, his grief was so great that he ignored the needs of his army and the soldiers came close to deserting him (see 2 Sam. 19:1–8).

In this final image of David as the father of his family, it's difficult to remember him as the golden hero we spoke of at the beginning of this chapter. It isn't easy to believe that this David is the same man who sought God with all his heart, the man with whom God was pleased. It's difficult to believe that David is the patriarch of the family through whom God would bring the King of kings. Yet this is the same David—spiritually minded but emotionally inept. He is a man of God with feet of clay.

Chapter 2

Christian Families Are Dysfunctional Too

Family dysfunction is a powerful force that can affect families, communities, and even nations for generations! The tragedy of dysfunction in King David's family, for example, continued long after David, Bathsheba, Absalom, Amnon, and Tamar were dead. It affected Solomon and his children and eventually ran so deep that the nation of Israel could no longer function. Ultimately, the dysfunction in David's family in 900 B.C. led to the breakup of the nation of Israel, which did not reunite until 1947!

For years I knew about David, but was unaware of the painful, emotional struggles in the family. But one Sunday, as I sat in church and listened to Chuck Swindoll talk about David and his family, I suddenly began to see how dysfunctional and pain-ridden the family was. Then I drew a genogram of David's family—I drew a map of the family relationships. Genograms are helpful in understanding the dynamics of family relationships and often point out possible origins of family problems.

As I looked at David's genogram, I realized that the genograms of many families I counsel look similar to David's. His family faced many of the same struggles as the families

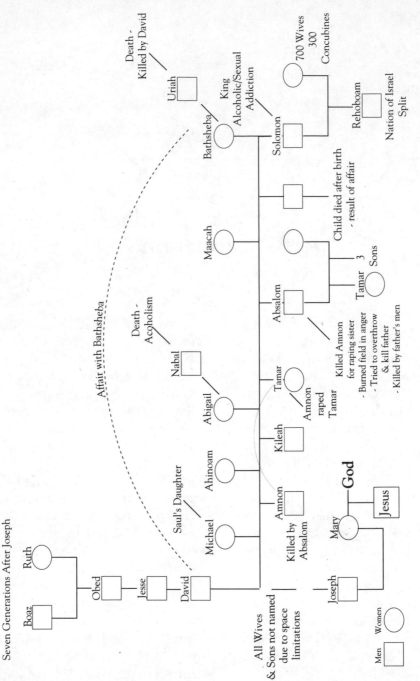

Seven Generations After Joseph

Affair with Bathsheba

Death - Killed by David

Uriah

Bathsheba

King Alcoholic/Sexual Addiction

Solomon

700 Wives
300 Concubines

Rehoboam

Nation of Israel Split

Child died after birth - result of affair

Maacah

Tamar   3 Sons

Absalom

Death - Alcoholism

Nabal

Abigail

Tamar

Amnon raped Tamar

Kileah

Killed Amnon for raping sister
- Burned field in anger
- Tried to overthrow & kill father
- Killed by father's men

Saul's Daughter

Ahinoam

God

Michael

Amnon

Mary

Jesus

Killed by Absalom

Joseph

Ruth

Obed

Boaz

Jesse

David

All Wives & Sons not named due to space limitations

Women

Men

I see in my counseling practice! In David's family we see first marriages, second marriages, deaths of spouses and young children, blended families, incest, rebellion, addiction, even murder! The specific details may vary, but what happened in David's family in 900 B.C. is very similar to what happens in families today.

I don't think God made a divine mistake by revealing that David—spiritual giant that he was—had family problems. I think the story of David's family shows that God has a far greater understanding of and concern for our most intimate family relationships than we realize. Furthermore, I believe He wants to heal us from the pain of those relationships. Thus the reality of emotional pain revealed through David's family life is a reality that we can identify with, a reality that can lead us into our own recovery.

The Reality of Family Dysfunction

The day-to-day realities of life in dysfunctional families are similar, whether the families lived 3,000 years ago or live today, whether the families are Christian or nonChristian. Let's look at some characteristics of dysfunctional families and how those characteristics are lived out in daily life.

Dysfunctional family members manipulate situations and go to great lengths to cover up problems rather than face them.   We saw this tendency clearly in David's numerous attempts to manipulate Uriah to cover up David's adulterous relationship with Bathsheba. Parents today use guilt and shame to get a desired response from their young children or even their adult children. Manipulative comments often take the form of statements such as, "I guess your father and I will be alone this Thanksgiving. I suppose you will have a wonderful time visiting your friends this holiday!" Another common practice in dysfunctional families is to get children to express one parent's emotional needs to the other parent instead of the parents dealing directly with each other.

Dysfunctional family members may develop psychosomatic illnesses.   Amnon became physically sick because of his desire to have sexual relations with his sister Tamar. Many illnesses today, perhaps as many as eighty percent, can be attributed to stress and unresolved emotional problems within the family. This is not to say that feelings are the exclusive cause of disease, but they do have an impact on disease. For example, a child with asthma who lives in a high-stress family will generally have more frequent asthma attacks than a child from a more nurturing family.

Dysfunctional family members handle pain by avoidance or denial.   David took the route of denial in handling his affair with Bathsheba. It took a direct confrontation with God's prophet Nathan to force David out of denial. Families today have a strong tendency to admit that things aren't perfect, but that they aren't bad enough to make a difference. A woman may convince herself that, even though her husband rages at their children, the children appear to be fine, so his abuse must not be too bad.

Dysfunctional family members suffer from improper spiritual, physical, emotional, or relational boundaries.   Amnon violated Tamar's physical, emotional, and spiritual boundaries when he raped her. Absalom violated a relational boundary when he assumed his father's responsibility for what was happening in the family. Boundary violations occur in families today when one partner blows up in anger at the other. Spiritual and emotional boundaries are also violated when parents tell their children that God doesn't like them when they don't do what their parents want them to do.

Dysfunctional family members are emotionally reactive rather than responsive.   We know that David was furious—an emotional reaction—about what happened to Tamar. Yet we see no evidence that he took action to resolve the situation. In families today, parents may become angry when a child doesn't keep his or her room picked up, but they may never teach the child how to do it. Emotional reactions of this kind are damaging to the child.

Dysfunctional family members try to promote change through behavior rather than direct communication. Instead of approaching David directly about the family problem, Absalom attempted to bring the whole family—including David—together for a celebration. Perhaps Absalom thought that if they could just get together, something good would happen. In the same way, a father today may think he is showing love for his family by working hard to bring in money, but he may never realize that he needs to communicate his love by expressing his feelings and being available for a hug.

Dysfunctional family members may break off communication with the person with whom they have conflict. Absalom refused to even speak to Amnon because of what Amnon did to Tamar. Suffering greatly, Tamar cut herself off from the outside world. Family members today may refuse to speak to each other or may move to different parts of the country to escape one or more of the other family members. They may also act out their emotional cutoffs by not allowing grandparents to visit their grandchildren or by preventing former spouses from developing meaningful relationships with their children.

Dysfunctional family members need to have a scapegoat. Absalom was clearly the scapegoat in David's family. By acting out the pain everyone else felt, he received the blame for his problems, plus the blame that belonged elsewhere. It is not uncommon for families today to place all the blame for family dysfunction on an angry and rebellious teenager who may be merely acting out feelings that no one else in the family is willing to deal with openly.

Dysfunctional family members create increasingly serious crises to communicate their pain. Absalom simply could not keep his feelings locked in. He created crisis after crisis—murdering Amnon, setting Joab's field on fire, causing Israel to rebel against David—in vain attempts to get the family to resolve the real problem. Today girls in dysfunctional families may develop eating disorders as a way of coping with the tension and their depression. These disorders may lead to serious symptoms, such as fainting or irregular heartbeat, that require hospitalization. Sadly, some parents don't realize that a family problem exists until a child is hospitalized.

Dysfunctional family members hope that time will heal the problems. After Tamar was raped, Absalom waited two years before he murdered Amnon, spent three years in exile, waited two more years, but the problem still was not resolved. He died waiting for the problem to get better. Unfortunately, time does nothing to fix family problems; it only allows unresolved problems to become more serious. Today, husbands or wives may ignore the little hurts, pretending that they don't matter, or that they will be dealt with later. Often, however, those hurts are never dealt with, and the distance and resentment keep on growing, perhaps leading to divorce.

Unfortunately, not one of these ways of dealing with problems in family relationships does the job. In fact, most of these methods encourage the problems to become worse. Unless family members recognize the dysfunction in their relationships and deal with it effectively, real change cannot occur.

Christian Families Aren't Immune From Dysfunction

Just as David's family had difficulty facing unpleasant family issues, many Christian families today find it hard to admit the possibility of dysfunctional family relationships. For some reason we tend to equate emotional dysfunction with spiritual deficiency. Yet the story of David's family ought to convince us otherwise. It's hard to find a man with a more admirable relationship with God than David, but he clearly headed a dysfunctional family.

Sometimes Christians assume that dysfunction only occurs in other families—families in which alcoholism, addiction, and physical abuse are part of daily life. Nothing could be further from the truth. Remember, dysfunctional families are not bad families. Dysfunctional families simply have trouble handling emotion. They may be unable to express their emotions. They may deny their feelings and problems. They may blame others for their feelings. Or they may express emotion in ways that are out of proportion with the immediate situation.

Christians also tend to believe that if the whole family goes to church happily on Sunday and maintains reasonably "Christian" behavior throughout the week, everything is fine. This, too, is a false belief. We can put great pressure on ourselves to conform to a nice, spiritually acceptable appearance even when our hearts are aching with pain. The sad truth is that we need healing in order to deal with the harsh realities of life, not conformity to a standard of perfection that denies reality.

I'd like to use my own family as an example of how easy it is for a God-fearing, "model" Christian family to be dysfunctional. Please realize that as I share the dysfunctional aspects of my family, I also recognize the many good experiences and values my family provided. I do not share our pain in an effort to cast blame, but to help you better understand family relationships and gain knowledge that will help you in your personal growth.

My family has a strong Christian heritage. Both of my parents came from hard-working Christian families that were highly respected in the community. Each member of my family believes in God and has accepted Jesus Christ as Lord and Savior. Yet for generations, on both sides, my family has had incredible difficulty dealing with feelings. It didn't matter if the feelings were anger, hurt, or happiness— they were all hard to face. To show you how difficult it was for us to deal with our feelings, or any type of emotional expression, let me share what happened when we received our first hug.

I was in my early teens. I remember standing in the front yard with my grandparents and parents, waiting for my uncle and his fiancée to arrive. We were waiting in the shade of my favorite tree, a giant maple with a trunk at least six feet around and limbs that stretched out to shade the whole front yard. I always looked forward to my uncle's visits. It seems as if he always had a new car—usually a blue Ford Thunderbird. (This was long before European and Japanese sports cars had stolen the hearts of American teenagers!) We watched as he drove up the long driveway toward our two-story farmhouse, a swirl of dust billowing out from under the car.

As the car rolled to a stop, my uncle jumped out and opened the door for his wife-to-be. Right away I noticed something unusual about her. She had a bright, bubbly smile! I wasn't used to seeing such a smile among the straight-faced Germans, Norwegians, and Swedes who made up our Minnesota farming community. Then she did something even more unusual. With a lively step, she quickly walked up to my grandfather and gave him a big hug!

I was fascinated. I'd never seen that happen before. An attractive young woman just walked up to my grandfather and hugged him! She had no idea that she broke nearly a hundred years of family rules when she gave him that hug! It didn't fit in our family at all. As I watched, my grandfather went straight as a board!

Then my aunt-to-be gave my grandmother a big hug. My grandmother had asthma and emphysema, and she began to wheeze and cough as soon as she was hugged. She had to pull out her aspirator and inhale some medication so she could breathe normally again!

Next it was my mom's turn. Her reaction was similar to my grandfather's. She stiffened, but her brow also wrinkled, which usually meant that a headache was on the way.

My father's response was entirely different. When my

uncle's fiancée hugged him, he held on like a camel that had found an oasis in the middle of the desert! She had to peel his hands off her.

Finally it was my turn. There I was, a teenager in the heat of adolescence, and a pretty, smiling woman gave me a big hug. I thought I'd died and gone to heaven! This is the first hug I remember. It was a new thing to receive a warm hug without having to ask or do something special to deserve it!

Facing the Reality of Dysfunction

Like it or not, my God-fearing, Christian family was dysfunctional. We had so little skill in handling our emotions that we didn't even know what to do with a hug! Yet that hug made a lasting impact. For me, God became a little more real that day. To me, that hug was a symbol of God's unconditional love—a love that did not require a particular performance from me. Other members of my family were also touched by the warm embrace.

My uncle later married the woman who introduced hugs into our family, and I could always look forward to a hug whenever they came to visit. After about five years of her influence, hugs became a regular part of our family experience. She once told me, "Earl, hug your family while they live so you will have no regrets when they die; they are impossible to embrace then." Now when I visit my brothers, sister, and parents, we greet each other with hugs. The day my aunt-to-be reached out to us, she initiated a very special change in our family.

The change was probably long overdue. From the stories I have heard about previous generations of my family, I know I come from a long line of hard-working Germans. For generations we kept our feelings inside, were rarely warm, and died from heart attacks—attacks of hearts that were never allowed to feel or share the burdens they carried. My family has long been one of the foundational families in the local church and has earned the respect of neighbors and others in the community. We have also kept our pain to ourselves as our members grew increasingly distant and detached.

Although alcoholism and drug addiction were unheard of in my family, we were familiar with other equally compulsive and destructive behaviors—overwork, overeating, excessive anger, and periodic physical and emotional abuse. We worked together well, exploring creative options to repair farm equipment or to help the business grow and prosper. Yet we couldn't begin to handle relational problems. Competent as we were in farming, we had no mechanism by which we could resolve family conflict.

Lacking the knowledge of how to deal with our problems, we did the best we could: We lived as if our problems did not exist. No one outside the family could have imagined the pain and conflict that were always brewing below the surface. Conflicts were never settled. Arguments were never resolved. Hurt was never worked out. Issues were silently stuffed deep inside until the next conflict blew everything up again.

Shame! The Fuel That Feeds Dysfunction

Shame is one of the primary reasons families have trouble dealing with emotions. Simply stated, shame is a deep feeling of worthlessness, inadequacy, and failure. We may feel shamed deep inside ourselves or may shame another person by using words or actions that make that person feel inadequate or worthless. In part two of this book, we will explore in much greater depth the role of shame in dysfunctional families, codependency, and addiction. For now, we need only to recognize that shame is a particularly potent force in dysfunctional Christian families.

Shame is a powerful force because shame-based families feel that admitting their pain or expressing a need for help means that they are "bad." Thus shame encourages us to keep deep secrets and avoid talking openly about family problems. In my family, for example, attempts to resolve conflicts were set up as "I win, you lose" situations. Conflicts were not efforts to establish a basis of understanding so that a satisfactory compromise could be reached. Instead, conflicts were like trials; whoever yelled the loudest or became the angriest won.

In addition, the discipline in my home was shame-based. When my brothers and sister and I misbehaved, we often received a cold look of shame. Instead of teaching us what we had done wrong and how we could correct our behavior, those shaming looks, accompanied by emotional distancing, made it clear that we were bad. If we did something bad enough that we had to be disciplined, the discipline was often too harsh, which only added to our shame. Yet my parents were only doing what they had learned in their families. They were only repeating what had been modeled to them as appropriate. In a way, what they expressed toward us was better than what they had experienced. What I then carried with me into my marriage and my relationship with my children, I had to become responsible for changing. I would be shaming in my interaction with my family. I had begun to pass on what had been passed on for generations.

Unfortunately my family experience isn't particularly unusual. Strong Christian families are often shame-based, especially if their church background emphasizes God's condemnation and judgment rather than Christ's grace and forgiveness. For a time my family was very involved in a shame-based church, where even the Bible was used as a weapon of shame rather than a beacon of God's grace and love. I'm not saying that it was a "bad" church, but it was a church in which religious shame was the norm. The church was full of nice people who sought God's will in the best way they knew how yet were stuck in a dysfunctional system that had been going on for generations.

The attitudes of religious shame prevalent in the church today make it very difficult for Christians to get the help they need. Churches need to actively correct the misconception that accepting Jesus Christ as Lord and Savior means that we are healed from all our trouble. Yes, Christians are forgiven and have been released by God from guilt and shame. Yes, some Christians are immediately healed and delivered from the grip of alcoholism, drug addiction, eating disorders, or other compulsive diseases. However, most Christians still have difficulty handling their emotions; most still have to recover from deep hurts; most still have to face the reality of compulsive diseases in their lives. So most of us need to grasp tightly the hand of our Savior as we work through a recovery process that will bring healing to our hearts.

It's time for the church to become a partner in this process rather than an obstacle, because the combination of family shame and religious shame is deadly. It keeps raging feelings locked up tightly inside people and unconsciously sets a tense, defensive tone for all family interaction. In my case, shame made it difficult for me to have a normal conversation with my parents. It seemed that tension and conflict was part of almost every interaction with them. In addition to these relational difficulties, I personally struggled with deep depression.

We must remember that emotional dysfunction is rarely the result of deficient spirituality. Rather, emotional dysfunction reflects our deep need to resolve the issues and heal the hurt we have suffered. Sadly, as in many families, the religious shame my family experienced simply fueled our denial instead of moving us toward recovery. Powerful force that it is, shame was the primary factor that kept my family living in deep, unresolved pain for generations.

To Live in Dysfunction Is to Live in Pain

My grandfather and grandmother, who were so stunned by a warm embrace, are now dead. I sometimes wonder about the deep pain they must have carried inside to have had such dramatic reactions to a loving, caring hug. I know, although they never talked about it, they had stuffed their pain deep inside. They grew up in a time with a family in which feelings were not discussed and expressions of caring just did not happen. They had no chance to learn that their family experiences could be different.

I remember my grandparents as kind, loving people. I know they wanted the best for their daughter, my mom, and for me. They truly loved us in the best way they knew how. Yet families pay a great price when feelings are forced underground. Although my grandparents' intentions were good, their inability to deal with emotions caused much pain for my parents and their siblings, which in turn led to pain for my brothers, sister, cousins, and me.

The sad truth is the dysfunction in our family caused us to miss out on many opportunities for celebration, happiness, and joy. I can remember what good students, athletes, and musicians the children of my generation were. But I can hardly remember receiving praise or encouragement. I'm sure we were praised and encouraged. I'm sure we had some fun times together. But the good memories seem to be tarnished by pain—wiped out by the more frequent, intense explosions of anger and the cold shoulder of shame.

I know my parents did the best they knew how to do. I know they loved me then and love me today. I know they both worked hard and sacrificed dearly so that each of their children would have the opportunity to become what we are today. I also know my parents grew up in families in which it wasn't possible to talk about feelings or to learn how to be close. As a result our family has had to deal with difficult communication, depression, compulsive overwork, overeating, episodic raging, and emotional distancing.

My great-grandparents did the best they could. My grandparents improved on what they did. And I admire and respect my parents for improving as well. Now it is my turn to improve on what those before me have done, so that my children will be able to move toward increasing health and closeness within their future families.

No matter who we are—a Minnesota farm family, a royal family in the ancient Middle East, a pastor's family, or the family of an alcoholic—we pay a dear price when we refuse to deal with family dysfunction. When we, often unconsciously, try to protect the secrets and deny our pain, we often hurt those we love. It's far easier to dump our anger or frustration on a spouse or child than to face the roots of these emotions. But when we remain in denial, we participate in our own emotional suicide or serve as an accomplice to the death of family relationships.

As we drift further and further away from functional relationships, we need more and more food, work, alcohol, sex, drugs, television, Christian service, or massive codependence to silence our hidden pain. These compulsions only increase the dysfunction and magnify the problems. In the next chapter we'll see how Solomon, another child of David's, tried to silence the pain of living in his dysfunctional family.

Chapter 3

Solomon: A Classic Victim
Of a Dysfunctional Family

The story of David, Amnon, Absalom, and Tamar gave us a good picture of how a dysfunctional family operates. We saw the complexity, confusion, and distress that reign in a family where relationships don't work. Now we will turn our focus from the interplay of relationships in a dysfunctional family to the effect family dysfunction can have on one individual. We'll take a close look at Solomon, an adult who grew up in a dysfunctional family.

Solomon was remarkable: incredibly wise, unimaginably wealthy, and immensely powerful. He was also a sensitive and expressive writer who made a significant contribution to Scripture. He wrote three books of the Bible—Proverbs, Song of Solomon, and Ecclesiastes—that give us insight into how adults live with the pain of growing up in a dysfunctional family. These writings also show some of the ways God can help people deal with emotional pain.

Solomon's book of Proverbs is filled with wisdom and guidelines for righteous living. It admonishes us to make right choices in spite of deep-rooted inner feelings that may be pulling us toward wrong choices and tragedy. The Song of Solomon is a poetic exploration of romantic and sexual love. It reflects Solomon's personal struggle in this area, a struggle faced by all too many adults from dysfunctional families. Finally, Solomon wrote Ecclesiastes. I like to think of it as Solomon's mid-life journal. It is a touching, and at times gut-wrenching, book that reveals the depth of Solomon's pain as well as the insight he gained when his personal life fell apart.

Let's turn our attention to Solomon's fascinating writings to discover what we can learn about him. Let's see what he shows us about life in a dysfunctional family and how an adult from a dysfunctional family handles life.

The Joy of Being David's Youngest Son

It appears that Solomon, David's youngest son and heir to his throne, was privileged to have a closer relationship with David than his older siblings experienced. Scripture records only three face-to-face meetings between David and his sons Absalom and Amnon. They each approached David for permission to meet with other family members, but scriptural accounts reveal no personal interaction beyond the basic communication required to request and grant permission. After Amnon's death, David cut off all communication with Absalom. Only by creating a crisis (burning Joab's barley field) was Absalom even permitted to see David's face. David and Absalom then had a face-to-face meeting, but Absalom's subsequent actions show that deep communication between father and son was lacking.

Some of Solomon's writings in Proverbs, however, reveal a deeper level of father/son communication than we might expect from these examples of David's fathering. For example, Proverbs 4:3–9 portrays David teaching Solomon about the importance of wisdom.

> When I was a boy in my father's house,
>   still tender, and an only child of my
>   mother,
> he taught me and said,
>   "Lay hold of my words with all your heart;
>   keep my commands and you will live.
> Get wisdom, get understanding. . . .

> *Esteem her, and she will exalt you;*
> *embrace her, and she will honor you.*
> *She will set a garland of grace on your head*
> *and present you with a crown of splendor."*

Can you picture Solomon as a young child, sitting at David's feet or walking hand-in-hand with him, listening to every word his father says? As we read Proverbs, we see many references to father/son relationships and many wise teachings that are prefaced with the words, "Listen, my son."

In 1 Kings 2:2–4 we also see evidence of heartfelt communication between father and son as David directs his final words to Solomon. He begins with, "I am about to go the way of all the earth," in the acknowledgment that his earthly life was ending.

> *So be strong, show yourself a man, and observe what the LORD your God requires: Walk in his ways, and keep his decrees and commands, his laws and requirements, as written in the Law of Moses so that you may prosper in all you do and wherever you go, and that the LORD may keep his promise to me: "If your descendants watch how they live, and if they walk faithfully before me with all their heart and soul, you will never fail to have a man on the throne of Israel."*

It's refreshing to see this level of caring communication between David and Solomon after reading about the trauma-filled relationships between David and his older children. However, the relational turmoil of the family dysfunction still played a great role in Solomon's development. As he grew older, Solomon found it increasingly difficult to deal with the pain in his heart and life. Consequently he developed numerous destructive behaviors.

Even at Its Best, Life in a Dysfunctional Family Is Painful

Try to imagine what it must have been like for young Solomon to witness the dysfunctional relationships in his

family. Imagine yourself hearing the whisperings of servants and other family members and piecing together the
fact that your father had had your mother's first husband
killed. What do you think when you learn that God allowed
a baby to die because of what your father did? Imagine your
confusion as you see your older sister's despair and hear of
your father's fury! Imagine your fear when you learn that
the servants of your older brother Absalom have murdered
Amnon. Which of those brothers was your favorite, the one
who'd race through the palace garden with you perched
high on his shoulders? Imagine what it felt like to flee Jerusalem with your parents because Absalom had gathered an
army that threatened to destroy your father and his kingdom!

Can you now begin to understand the raging emotions
that Solomon must have felt just from living in his family?
Who would he have talked to in order to understand what
was happening? How would he have handled the discrep-
ancy of feeling secure when his father talked to him about
wisdom, law, and obeying God, but then being afraid to talk
about the mixed-up feelings that haunted him deep inside?
Is it any wonder that Solomon, when he had the chance,
asked God to give him wisdom?

Like so many others who grow up in dysfunctional families, Solomon internalized raging emotions. Try as he
might, he couldn't keep the hurt down deep enough or run
far enough away from it. In his adult life he lived out the
hurt that had accumulated since childhood. Ecclesiastes
2:1–16 chronicles the many ways he attempted to rid himself of pain. Some of them may sound very familiar to you.

• He filled himself with pleasure, laughter, wine, and
foolishness.
• He undertook great projects, building gardens, parks,
and reservoirs.
• He amassed more wealth—slaves, livestock, silver,
gold—than anyone in Jerusalem had ever accumulated.
• He bought himself every pleasure—entertainers and
even a harem.

• He educated himself.
• He had an absolute commitment to refuse himself no pleasure.

Solomon achieved the American dream thousands of years before the United States existed! But when he had done it all, he realized that he felt no better than before. Pleasure was worthless. Work was futile. Wisdom was meaningless.

No matter what he did or how well he did it, Solomon suffered the pain of growing up in a dysfunctional family. Like many other adults from dysfunctional families, he tried to escape that pain. He tried everything under the sun to avoid the storm within. As a result, his life demonstrates the same codependent, compulsive, and addictive behaviors that plague adults from dysfunctional families today. Let's look at Solomon's life and see how he lived out these characteristic behaviors.

Adults from Dysfunctional Families Generally Overachieve or Underachieve

Adults from dysfunctional families have a tendency toward extreme levels of achievement. Rarely average, they usually overachieve or underachieve. Solomon opted for excessive achievement. He built a fabulous temple for the Lord and a massive palace for himself. He built houses, parks, gardens, and reservoirs (Eccl. 2:4–6). In addition to his construction projects, Solomon was known for his knowledge and wisdom. First Kings 4:34 says, "Men of all nations came to listen to Solomon's wisdom, sent by all the kings of the world, who had heard of his wisdom." Solomon's wisdom encompassed a knowledge of plants, animals, birds, reptiles, and fish. In addition he "spoke three thousand proverbs and his songs numbered a thousand and five" (1 Kings 4:32).

That's quite a list of accomplishments! Nevertheless, Solomon described these achievements as "meaningless, a chasing after the wind" (Eccl. 2:11). He saw nothing but futility in all that he did. John of Salisbury, in his prologue to *Policraticus,* succinctly describes the frustration that Solomon and so many other adults from dysfunctional families face:

> The brevity of our life, the dullness of our senses, the torpor of our indifference, the futility of our occupation, suffer us to know but little: and that little is soon shaken and then torn from the mind by that traitor to learning, that hostile and faithless stepmother to memory, oblivion.[1]

What a tragedy to put so much of oneself into gaining knowledge and producing work, only to discover that such pursuits yield no ultimate meaning or satisfaction!

Adults from Dysfunctional Families Are Often Substance Abusers

Adults from dysfunctional families find creative ways to deaden their pain. They learn early that alcohol, drugs, or even food can take the edge off the pain deep inside and make life seem bearable. However, these comforting substances cause serious problems. First, they damage the body as they deaden the pain. Second, users usually need increasing amounts of these substances to keep the pain under control. Third, as long as the pain is medicated, the user will never face the problems that cause the pain.

Solomon's substance of choice was alcohol: "I tried cheering myself with wine" (Eccl. 2:3). It seems that he consumed excessive amounts of alcohol in an attempt to find solace for his despair. His description of the final stages of alcohol addiction, found in Proverbs 23:29–35, shows that he was intimately acquainted with the symptoms.

> *Who has woe? Who has sorrow?*
> *Who has strife? Who has complaints?*
> *Who has needless bruises? Who has*
> *bloodshot eyes?*
> *Those who linger over wine,*
> *who go to sample bowls of mixed wine.*

> *Do not gaze at wine when it is red,*
> *when it sparkles in the cup,*
> *when it goes down smoothly!*
> *In the end it bites like a snake*
> *and poisons like a viper.*
> *Your eyes will see strange sights*
> *and your mind imagine confusing things.*
> *You will be like one sleeping on the high seas,*
> *lying on top of the rigging.*
> *"They hit me," you will say, "but I'm not hurt!*
> *They beat me, but I don't feel it!*
> *When will I wake up*
> *so I can find another drink?"*

Solomon missed few symptoms of acute alcoholism in this description. He bemoans the psychological condition of the alcoholic—one of woe, sorrow, strife, and complaint. He describes the enticement of the drink, noting its color and how it feels going down. People who are not alcoholics are rarely so fascinated by the color, sparkle, or smooth character of wine. He obviously has felt the downside of alcohol, too—the bizarre hallucinations, the confusion of mental and emotional disorientation, the seemingly endless bouts of nausea, and the bewilderment of numbed physical senses. At the end, he expresses the desire for yet another drink; he is obsessed with the need for another drink to anesthetize the unbearable pain within.

Adults from Dysfunctional Families Find Intimacy Difficult

Solomon struggled with intimacy. As a classic over-achiever, he gave intimate relationships his best shot. Scripture tells us he acquired 700 wives and 300 concubines (see 1 Kings 11:3). Obviously he opted for quantity rather than quality!

Several of Solomon's writings reveal his struggle for intimacy. The Song of Solomon portrays an intimate relationship that did not last. Ecclesiastes 4:9–12 reveals a longing for intimacy—a longing for the warmth, strength, and support of an intimate partner. Throughout Proverbs, Solomon admonishes his readers to cling to one's spouse and maintain sexual fidelity. Toward the end of his life, we see Solomon scrambling to please his many wives and thereby maintain some harmony in his home. First Kings 11:4–8 shows Solomon building temples to the gods of all his wives, perhaps hoping that he could please them and have the intimacy he so desperately wanted.

Perhaps, too, Solomon's many wives and concubines reveal another addiction—sexual addiction. Although it was culturally acceptable to have a harem and to marry for political reasons, Solomon certainly didn't need 1,000 sexual partners to become socially and politically respectable! Perhaps he lessened the pain of his disappointing intimate relationships by having a great quantity and variety of relationships.

Despite the fact that Solomon was literally surrounded by wives, concubines, and servants, he often expressed his loneliness. Ecclesiastes 4:8 portrays a hard-working man without a son or a brother who realized that working for money was worthless and that intimate, abiding relationships were more valuable. Intimacy must have been a deep longing for Solomon. It is tragic that the wisest man on earth turned from woman to woman yet never found the intimacy he so desperately wanted.

It is common for adults from dysfunctional families to feel loneliness and to do almost anything to avoid those feelings. That is why codependency is such an important issue for adults from dysfunctional families. When we become obsessed with another person, we don't have to face the nagging loneliness within.

Adults from Dysfunctional Families Have Trouble Expressing and Focusing Their Feelings

From beginning to end, the word *meaningless* jumps out from the pages of Ecclesiastes: "This, too, is meaningless"; "This is meaningless, a chasing after the wind"; and "Again I saw something meaningless under the sun." Solomon was ultimately frustrated in every aspect of life. He lived through years of accomplishments, struggles, and disappointments, but worst of all, he considered everything he did to be meaningless.

When a person has tried everything and achieved all that can be achieved, despair and meaninglessness seem to follow close behind. That was Solomon's struggle. He did everything. He accomplished great things, made great contributions to the nation of Israel, and indulged himself in every pleasure imaginable. Then he reached a point where there really wasn't anything more to do. But more importantly, he realized that nothing he had done came close to touching the emptiness in his heart; he felt the meaninglessness of his life with its full impact.

The sad truth is: There are dimensions of emptiness that by ourselves we cannot fill. There is a dimension of emptiness that is filled only when we share our hurt with God and others who love us. There is a certain dimension of emptiness that only God can fill. If we try to fill our emptiness with substitutes, the result is meaninglessness.

Adults from Dysfunctional Families Often Choose Destructive Relationships

God specifically told the Israelites not to marry certain foreign women "because they will surely turn your hearts after their gods" (1 Kings 11:2). So what did wise King Solomon do? He married them—as many as he could. He first married Pharaoh's daughter. Afterward he married Moabites, Ammonites, Edomites, Sidonians, and Hittites! And, just as God said they would, they turned Solomon's heart away from God. In fact, Solomon so completely rejected God that He took the kingdom away from Solomon's family (see 1 Kings 11:9–13).

You would think that the man to whom God gave His wisdom would have known better than to make such destructive personal choices. Unfortunately this was not the case. Solomon, just like other adults from dysfunctional families, made his choices on the basis of deep (and probably unconscious) feelings. He repeated some of the same mistakes his forebearers made—mistakes that he probably vowed never to repeat.

Adults from Dysfunctional Families Often Do The Opposite of What They Know Is Right

Solomon—son of David, who diligently sought God with all his heart—made many choices that took him further and further away from God. As a young king, Solomon had ample opportunity and encouragement to make the right choices. God even appeared to Solomon in a dream and offered to give him anything he wanted (see 1 Kings 3:4–14). At that time Solomon made the right choice, asking for wisdom and discernment in governing God's people. God gave him that *and much more* because it was a good choice.

As time went on, however, Solomon did not continue to make good choices. He chose sex, alcohol, study, great projects, pleasure—seemingly everything but God! His compulsiveness seems to have progressed to an addictive cycle of alcoholism and sexual addiction. As those diseases advanced, Solomon's life became more and more out of control. He eventually lost his ability to make choices and sustain changes; his addictions made his choices for him.

Adults from Dysfunctional Families Have Difficulty with Consistent Relationships—Even with God

We know that Solomon didn't have consistent, intimate relationships with women. He compulsively turned from one relationship to the next. One would have thought that he could have maintained a consistent relationship with God, but that was not the case.

Solomon had a lot going for him spiritually. He was David's son, and despite David's relational problems, David certainly provided a worthy spiritual model to emulate. Like his father, Solomon started out with a powerful relationship with God. Solomon built God's temple in Jerusalem and was king of Israel at the high point of the nation's spiritual life. God personally appeared to him in dreams on two different occasions. God even told Solomon exactly what He expected of their relationship:

> As for you, if you walk before me in integrity of heart and uprightness, as David your father did, and do all I command and observe my decrees and laws, I will establish your royal throne over Israel forever, as I promised David your father. . . . But if you or your sons turn away from me and do not observe the commands and decrees I have given you and go off to serve other gods and worship them, then I will cut off Israel from the land I have given them and will reject this temple I have consecrated for my Name. Israel will then become a byword and an object of ridicule among all peoples. (1 Kings 9:4–7)

Yet all of this wasn't enough to maintain a faithful relationship with God for the duration of Solomon's life. Later in life, Solomon "did evil in the eyes of the LORD" (1 Kings 11:6). Solomon knew better than to abandon God's ways. He even wrote about the importance of obeying God but was unable to put what he knew into action in his own life. When his relationship with God deteriorated, everything else was lost.

Adults from Dysfunctional Families Have A Childlike Part of Themselves

Solomon was aware of the childlike part of himself. When God appeared to Solomon the first time and offered to give him anything, Solomon asked God to address that area of weakness. He said, "I am only a little child and do not know how to carry out my duties" (1 Kings 3:7).

Imagine: Even with the instruction David had given Solomon, he still felt like a small, vulnerable child who could not do the job. Many adults from dysfunctional families face similar inordinate fear about their ability to succeed. Even though their abilities may earn them high positions, they may be haunted by unfounded fear of failure. In addition, they may at times exhibit emotions that are typically expressed by young children—pouting, sulking, and even temper tantrums. All of these feelings are signs of hurt or anger that come from one's family of origin and need to be dealt with properly.

Adults from Dysfunctional Families Want Quick, Painless Results

God granted Solomon's request for wisdom. It was a painless solution to the fearsome incompetence Solomon felt inside. But the gift of wisdom did not resolve all of Solomon's inadequacies. He still had other problems and issues to work through, which he refused to do. Instead he applied huge doses of alcohol, women, and work to anesthetize the problems and the pain. By doing so, he avoided both God and his family. In time, his addictions rendered his wisdom ineffective and halted his spiritual growth.

Solomon was so desperate for quick, easy results— healthy relationships, power, success, love—that two face-to-face appearances with God did not put him on the right track. He realized too late that he had avoided the issues that really mattered: having a close walk with God, providing spiritual leadership for his family, and living a godly lifestyle. Because Solomon refused to deal with the real issues and make God's priorities his own, God took the kingdom away from Solomon's heirs.

Today quick results are the norm. Our technological society keeps moving us at a faster and faster pace. We microwave meals because we cram more activity into a day than we can stand. We fax information because it might take a day or two to get through the mail. Don't get me wrong, I use a microwave, a fax machine, and a computer. But when it comes to relationships, I must continually remind myself that quick results aren't the answer. People don't change at the push of a button. It takes time and effort to deal with the important issues, to face the feelings inside so that we can have healthy relationships with God and family.

Adults from Dysfunctional Families
Have Difficulty Handling Success

The high point of influence for the nation of Israel occurred during Solomon's reign. The surrounding nations paid tribute to Israel; the people of Israel ate, drank, and were happy (see 1 Kings 4:20). From one end of the nation to the other, people lived in peace and safety, "each man under his own vine and fig tree" (1 Kings 4:25). The ancient version of the American dream was fulfilled. Everyone had the equivalent of a car in the garage and a chicken in the pot!

The benefits of Solomon's reign were not limited to the comforts of peace and the accumulation of material wealth. Solomon's reign also marked Israel's spiritual zenith. He accomplished the construction, dedication, and consecration of the temple of the Lord. When the ark was brought into the temple, the cloud of God's presence was so great that the priests had to leave! They couldn't even do what they were supposed to do. There has never been a greater day of fear, joy, and excitement in the history of Israel!

No doubt about it, Solomon achieved almost unbelievable success. But it didn't last. At the end of his life, he turned his back on God; he was too busy building temples for his wives' gods. Like many of us, he forgot that his relationship with God was the most important one and he allowed other things to take first place.

Adults from Dysfunctional Families Tend To
Perpetuate the Problems of Their Families

Solomon, the wisest man who ever lived, never gained an understanding of the emotional issues that controlled his life. As a result, he merely perpetuated the dysfunctional ways of living that he learned as a child. The same is true of adults from dysfunctional families today. The great temptation is to deny the dysfunction, which only gives it free reign to increase in subsequent generations.

For example, David's violation of marriage (his affair

with Bathsheba) threatened his relationship with God and had a long-term impact on his children. The marriages of adult children often reflect the marriages of their parents. In Solomon's case, his violation of marriage (choosing to marry women God had commanded him not to marry) seems to be the most powerful influence in destroying his relationship with God.

By the time Solomon's son Rehoboam became king, Solomon's foreign wives had become the dominant spiritual force in the nation. The royal household, as well as the whole tribe of Judah, had abandoned its relationship with God. "There were even male shrine prostitutes in the land; the people engaged in all the detestable practices of the nations the LORD had driven out before the Israelites" (1 Kings 14:24). Male prostitutes came from the worship of other gods in the temples that Solomon built for his pagan wives. Solomon, the same man who built God's temple, also helped to bring such degradation to God's people.

Rehoboam's actions in governing the nation of Israel also indicate that the emotional distance between father and son, which is evident in David's relationships, continued for generations. When Rehoboam became king, he rejected the counsel of his father's most trusted advisors (see 1 Kings 12:6–15). Instead of lightening the heavy tax burden that Solomon had placed on the people at the end of his reign, Rehoboam vowed to make the burden even heavier!

This was obviously a destructive choice, far more destructive than the poor choices his father, Solomon, had made. This one choice caused Israel to rebel against Rehoboam and the whole house of David! First Kings 12:16 even records the words of the people of Israel: "What share do we have in David, what part in Jesse's son? To your tents, O Israel! Look after your own house, O David!"

In three generations of rule by David's family, we see the nation uniting, living in peace, and then splitting apart. Just as David's family was shattered by its inability to handle emotion, so also the nation of Israel was fragmented and destroyed. The split was so traumatic that reconciliation between Israel and Judah—between the nation and the house of David—never took place.

The problems of dysfunctional families cannot get better on their own. Time only intensifies the pain and increases the devastation caused by unresolved family problems. The penalty of dysfunction increases with each generation!

Chapter 4

Abigail:
A Classic Codependent

Solomon exhibited behaviors that for thousands of years have characterized adults from dysfunctional families, behaviors that attempt to smother pain, behaviors that result from emotional or physical abuse, behaviors that result from underdeveloped emotions, behaviors that are destructive to oneself and others. All of these behaviors are responses to the pain of living in a dysfunctional family. All are responses of hurting people. All are responses of codependent people.

Dysfunctional families always produce hurting, codependent people. Depending on which behaviors people exhibit, and to what degree they exhibit them, we may refer to people as primarily codependent, compulsive, or addictive. But these terms are not absolute or exclusive.

As those of us who work in the psychological community have learned to deal with the complex problems of dysfunctional families, we have realized that all people are codependent to a greater or lesser degree. We have discovered that certain codependent people may at times develop compulsive behaviors such as overeating, perfectionism, or excessive work. We have also learned that when alcoholics and other addicts eliminate destructive substances from their lives, they often discover underlying codependency issues that must also be resolved.

For example, Solomon was in some ways codependent, at times compulsive, and clearly addicted. He built temples to the gods of his foreign wives in order to please them, even though he knew that building those temples would be destructive to him by separating him from God. Such an intense focus on pleasing others, even to the detriment of oneself, is typical of codependents. Solomon's compulsiveness is further demonstrated by his intense pursuit of knowledge and huge building projects. His writings reflect ample evidence of sexual and alcohol addictions.

Codependent, compulsive, and addictive behaviors typify the responses of adults who grew up with family dysfunction. Unfortunately, these behaviors do nothing to resolve the underlying issues. In fact, they are ultimately destructive, leading to yet another generation of family dysfunction and pain.

What's So Bad About Being Codependent?

It is easy for most people today to identify the destructive potential of alcoholism and other addictions. Many of us can identify the pain caused by compulsive behaviors. For instance, we can understand the pain a child feels when a workaholic father is never available to play ball, and we can see the burden that a mother's extreme perfectionism places on her children. However, particularly in Christian circles, it is often difficult for us to see the damaging potential of codependent behaviors. Here's why.

First, many Christians actually view codependent behaviors as virtuous! We often admire Christian codependents for their "unselfish" behavior. We respect the man who is always serving the church on this or that committee, even though he gives up his family time three or four nights a week to do so. We honor the woman who directs the toddler program—making sure the room is stocked with clean toys and staffed with happy workers, and that every child has a healthy snack—even if she's so busy that her own children long for a chance to play with her. We commend the single men and women who enthusiastically lead the youth program, not realizing that their involvement could be a convenient way to avoid the work of developing effective relationships with their adult peers.

Second, codependents are often well-adjusted, loving, caring people. Unfortunately they give up part of themselves to be this way. Codependents set aside their own needs and values in order to gain the approval of others; they give up part of themselves to be in relationships. They may feel guilty whenever they do something fun or special for themselves, even if it's something as necessary as taking time for proper rest. Although codependents may appear to be happy and loving, they harbor incredible pain and turmoil inside.

Part of the shame Christian codependents feel concerning caring for themselves comes from a mistaken view of Scripture that puts Jesus first, others second, and myself last. Yet it is hard for that view to stand up to Jesus' second commandment in Matthew 22:39: "Love your neighbor as *yourself.*"

Third, codependents can handle high levels of pain and craziness, appearing to handle difficult people and situations with saintly strength. Although they may eagerly meet the expectations of everyone who needs their help, they may be deeply angry that no one notices the great personal sacrifices they make. Furthermore, by going to such extremes to "help" others, codependents actually rob others of the growth opportunities that responsibilities and difficulties provide. For example, the parents who always bail out their adult children when they are short of money do themselves a disservice and aren't helping their children learn to handle finances properly.

Although the actions of codependents may appear far more benign than those of addictive or compulsive individuals, they are not. Like addicts and compulsive individuals, codependents are trying to patch up rather than resolve the pain of dysfunctional relationships. Some codependents do this by trying to control the behavior of others. Some do it by withdrawing and not creating problems for others. Others may do it by striving to please others. No matter what the method or how sincere and well-meaning the actions of codependents may be, codependent behavior is ultimately destructive—to the codependent as well as to those with whom the codependent has a close relationship.

Scripture tells the story of a classic codependent. Her name was Abigail. Her first husband was Nabal, an alcoholic. Her second husband was—you guessed it—King David! Her story begins in 1 Samuel 25:2. Let's see what we can learn about codependent living from her story.

Codependents May Appear to Have Everything, but Often Choose Problem-prone Relationships

At first glance, Abigail and Nabal seem to be the couple with everything. A wealthy rancher and property owner, he owned thousands of sheep and goats. She was intelligent and beautiful. Very soon, however, our perfect image of this couple shatters: "Her husband, a Calebite, was surly and mean in his dealings" (1 Sam. 25:3).

Wealth, intelligence, success, and beauty alone can't make a happy life. Nabal and Abigail appeared to have everything going for them, but they had problems,too. Success and financial security offer no protection against relational difficulties. Like Nabal and Abigail, we may gain everything the world has to offer, yet suffer turmoil and trouble in our marriages and family lives.

As the story progresses, we gain further insight into Nabal's lack of responsibility and arrogance (see 1 Sam. 25:4–11). It was sheep shearing time, and Nabal's shepherds had all they could do to shear his 3,000 sheep. David's men, who were in the area, protected Nabal's herds and supplies so that the shepherds could do their work without fear of attack by roving bands of thieves. At that time, it was normal for the owner of the herds to pay a gratuity to the men who protected them, but when David sent several of his men to request payment, Nabal insulted them and sent them away empty-handed.

Nabal's response to David's reasonable request was not only surly and mean, it was downright stupid! When David heard what had happened, he and 400 of his men armed themselves and began marching toward Nabal's estate to destroy it (see 1 Sam. 25:12–13). At this point in the story, Abigail's codependence becomes obvious:

> *One of the servants told Nabal's wife Abigail: "David sent messengers from the desert to give our master his greetings, but he hurled insults at them. Yet these men were very good to us. They did not mistreat us, and the whole time we were out in the fields near them nothing was missing. Night and day they were a wall around us all the time we were herding our sheep near them. Now think it over and see what you can do, because disaster is hanging over our master and his whole household. He is such a wicked man that no one can talk with him."*
> *(1 Sam. 25:14–17)*

Obviously past experiences had taught the servants exactly how things worked in the home. Nabal made things so difficult that he wasn't even worth talking to, but no matter how bad things got, Abigail could be counted on to come through! Nabal could be mean, he could be impossible to reason with, and he could shirk his responsibilities. But Abigail would make the personal sacrifices necessary to soothe the wounds, mend the fences, and keep the family functioning.

I believe Abigail lived this way because she was a codependent. As with the lives of so many other hurting people, her life consisted of caring for the emotional and physical needs of others. She knew of no other way to survive.

Although Scripture tells us nothing about Abigail's childhood, codependent people often come from dysfunctional families where they have had to care for one or both of their parents. Thus it is possible that Abigail was a "caretaker" from childhood, unintentionally groomed for a life partner whom she could "rescue" or "fix." Members of her family of origin also may have had difficulty being emotionally close or expressing their feelings. So living with someone like Nabal, who couldn't communicate with anyone, may have been a continuation of what seemed perfectly normal to her. It is also possible that Abigail learned to be codependent simply in order to survive in her marriage. Whatever the causes, Abigail exhibited classic codependent behavior.

Codependents Learn to Rescue The Family from Crisis

Nabal may not have cared about David or what he planned to do, but Abigail immediately recognized the seriousness of the crisis. As soon as the servant explained the situation, she sprang into action. Scripture says, "Abigail lost no time. She took two hundred loaves of bread, two skins of wine, five dressed sheep, five seahs of roasted grain, a hundred cakes of raisins and two hundred cakes of pressed figs, and loaded them on donkeys" (1 Sam. 25:18).

Codependents are great in a crisis. They are well prepared for nearly any emergency. Look at Abigail. More than likely, she had bailed Nabal out of trouble before. This time she was prepared to feed an army at a moment's notice—and she didn't even have a microwave!

The sad thing is that codependents almost always take on more responsibility in the family than they should. Often it is more responsibility than they want to have. Whenever they see problems in the family or marriage, codependents feel that all will be lost if they don't take control of the situation. For example, the codependent wife who cannot trust her alcoholic husband to use money responsibly will make sure the bills are paid. Often the only reason such families have a home is because the codependent has shouldered the responsibility.

Tragically, the harder codependents try to solve their problems, the more deeply enmeshed in those problems they become. For example, Abigail had stepped in for years to shore up Nabal's weaknesses and keep him out of trouble. As a result, his servants considered him to be totally inept. Instead of looking to Nabal for help, they turned to Abigail.

Although they may not realize it, codependents thrive on responsibility. When they work out solutions to extreme problems, they gain a false sense of self-worth. They feel a sense of worthiness that they generally do not feel otherwise. For example, shortly after we moved to California my wife, Karen, worked very hard to arrange a birthday party for me. In the middle of the party, I received a phone call from an extended family member who needed to talk. I listened, for forty-five minutes. By the time the call was over, everyone had gone home. I didn't value my own worth enough to say, "Look, I'm in the middle of my birthday party. I'll call you back in two hours." I couldn't even set aside a few hours to enjoy my own party.

Codependents Learn to Face Life Alone

When Abigail gathered all the food together, she and her servants set out toward David's camp. First Samuel 25:19 tells us that she didn't even tell Nabal what she was doing. She, like the servants, knew it was useless to talk with Nabal about the problem he had created. There was no point in wasting time arguing with him about the facts.

Abigail now faced a severe crisis—alone. Isolated, totally on her own, she prepared to face 400 men who had no objective other than to kill her entire family. Like many codependents, Abigail had long since lost any trace of support from her spouse. Facing problems alone—even life-threatening ones—had become routine.

Such feelings of isolation are common for codependents. At crucial times in life, when a hug, a warm smile, or a touch would communicate support and understanding, the codependent is alone. In times of need the codependent is left to nurse his or her hurts alone, without support from other family members. The codependent child learns it is useless to count on his or her alcoholic parents. The codependent husband or wife realizes the addicted spouse cannot function adequately in daily life; the codependent must handle all family responsibilities.

Codependents Assume Personal Responsibility For the Actions of Others

Abigail didn't consider her job done when she sent the food out to David's army. She went along to make sure that David's anger would be appeased. As she rode her donkey through the deep mountain ravine, David and his men ambushed her. We read about her face-to-face meeting with David in 1 Samuel 25:23–25:

> When Abigail saw David, she quickly got off her donkey and bowed down before David with her face to the ground. She fell at his feet and said: "My lord, let the blame be on me alone. Please let your servant speak to you; hear what your servant has to say. May my lord pay no attention to that wicked man Nabal. He is just like his name—his name is Fool, and folly goes with him. But as for me, your servant, I did not see the men my master sent."

Here we see another classic trait of codependents: Abigail assumed total responsibility for what Nabal had done. She begged David to blame her for the incident. She said that she was at fault because she should have seen David's men when they came to her home. She even judged herself guilty for an act she did not commit.

Like Abigail, codependents tend to feel responsible for everything that happens in the family. They feel guilty for everything that goes wrong, even if it has nothing to do with them. For example, a wife who has just been yelled at by her husband may decide that she needs to be more loving so he doesn't have to get so angry. In doing so, she takes responsibility for his anger. Chances are she will do whatever she needs to do so that he never has to face and deal with the reality of his anger. It's common for codependents to feel that if only they could change themselves or their way of doing things the problems in the family would not exist.

Instead of looking at situations and recognizing the legitimate responsibility each family member bears, codependents tend to shoulder all the responsibility. Therefore addicted family members, like Nabal, are never confronted with their responsibilities and never have to deal with the consequences of their failures. By assuming the responsibility and the burden of consequences that rightly belong to others, codependents actually enable addicted or otherwise dysfunctional family members to continue their destructive behaviors unabated. That is what happened to Abigail and Nabal.

Without Change, the Quality of Life For All Family Members Decreases

Codependents can be powerful people. David listened to Abigail's speech and granted her request. Her family was spared. She had stopped David in his tracks, something that thousands of Israel's enemies, including the giant Goliath, had failed to do. When Abigail returned home, however, things were just as bad as ever.

On the way Abigail must have rehearsed what she would say to Nabal. After all, he probably had no idea what David had almost done to him and his family. However, things did not go as she had planned: "When Abigail went to Nabal, he was in the house holding a banquet like that of a king. He was in high spirits and very drunk. So she told him nothing until daybreak" (1 Sam. 25:36).

Like many spouses and children of alcoholics, Abigail knew it wouldn't do any good to talk to Nabal when he was drunk. Perhaps he was most surly, mean, and insulting when he was drunk. So once again, after weathering a crisis that would leave anyone badly shaken, Abigail kept her feelings to herself. She was married, but she received no personal support from the relationship.

The next morning, when Nabal was sober, Abigail told him what happened. His response gives us insight into Nabal's behavior. Upon hearing Abigail's story, Nabal's "heart failed him and he became like a stone. About ten days later, the LORD struck Nabal and he died" (1 Sam. 25:37–38). We can surmise that Nabal was an alcoholic because we know that a person in the last stages of alcoholism can suffer a stroke, seizure, or heart attack while withdrawing from a bout of drunkenness. He also may have been in a coma during the ten days before his death.

No wonder there was turmoil in the family! An alcoholic family is a bit like a storm-swept ship on the ocean. Most of the time it is out of control, in constant danger of being swamped or capsized. While the captain of the ship (usually the codependent) fights for control, the passengers feel totally helpless; frightened, they wonder whether they will survive.

Many people have lived the same nightmare that Nabal's family lived. Many children have learned to wait until daddy is sober before daring to talk to him. Even then, those children have learned to be on guard because they never know when he will yell or belittle them in some unexpected way. In such families, the children and the spouse learn to tiptoe around the alcoholic in an often vain effort to keep peace. They know what it's like to never be able to count on Dad, to be embarrassed and humiliated by his drunken insults, and to live in the shadow of his intimidating presence.

Without positive change, life in a dysfunctional family gets worse and ultimately leads to death. Never forced to face his responsibilities, Nabal let Abigail carry the burdens alone until their marriage relationship existed for appearances only. Never confronted with his destructive addiction, Nabal kept it up until it killed him. Tragically, even though Nabal died, the damaging effects of his family relationships continued.

Without Change, the Effects of Dysfunctional Relationships Continue

When Nabal died, David rejoiced. He said, "Praise be to the LORD, who has upheld my cause against Nabal for treating me with contempt. He has kept his servant from doing wrong and has brought Nabal's wrongdoing down on his own head" (1 Sam. 25:39). Perhaps, Abigail, too, felt some relief. If so, her relief was short-lived.

David had been tremendously impressed with Abigail. After all, she was beautiful, competent, intelligent, and persuasive. When he heard that Nabal was dead, David jumped at the chance to have her as his wife. One would think that Abigail would have learned some things from her relationship with Nabal that would have helped her in future relationships. Her response to David, however, shows that was not the case: "She bowed down with her face to the ground and said, 'Here is your maidservant, ready to serve you and wash the feet of my master's servants'" (1 Sam. 25:41).

Abigail was all too used to serving. Serving others, even to her own detriment, was the only way she knew how to live. She not only offered herself as David's servant, but was willing to take care of his servants, too! Such an extreme degree of self-sacrifice went far beyond her obligation as a wife.

Although David offered the strength, kindness, and protection that Nabal had never provided, Abigail's troubles were by no means over. It was an honor to be the wife of a great warrior, but her marriage to David didn't lessen the pain of dysfunctional relationships in Abigail's life. Instead she found herself in another dysfunctional marriage, to be cast aside as David became fascinated with other women. Abigail had changed marriage partners, but she had not changed her codependent way of living, so the painful cycle merely continued.

The lesson is: Codependents will repeatedly find themselves in destructive relationships unless they make significant changes in themselves. Difficult as they are, those changes can be made. Although Abigail's options were somewhat limited by cultural norms, the limitations with which she lived do not exist today. Codependents can break the cycle of harmful relationships. Linda is an example of a codependent who was able to do so.

When Linda first came to my office for therapy, she told

me about her conflict-filled marriage. Her husband had had an affair and at one time moved out to live with his new-found love. Later he wanted to come back home and live with Linda. She agreed, on the condition that he enter a counseling program. He did but abandoned the program after only a few sessions. Linda continued counseling without him.

For years Linda had lived with her husband's alcoholism and emotional and physical abuse—at one time he had even held a gun to her head. For a long time she thought that if she could be a better person her husband would be better, too. Slowly she realized that no matter how many different ways she tried to change herself, she would not be safe in her marriage unless her husband sought help and changed, too. She began to understand her codependency: She continually tried to please a man who only related to women by controlling, dominating, and victimizing them. She realized his drinking always resulted in his emotional or physical abuse of her. Finally, because of the physical threat he posed, she divorced him.

Two years later Linda began to date again. She was excited about the new relationship until she discovered, to her amazement and dismay, that the new man of her dreams was also an alcoholic. Unlike many codependents, however, Linda had learned something from her marriage and had changed some of her codependent behavior. This time she wasn't afraid to talk about vital relationship issues. When she did, however, the man she was dating distanced himself from her and later ended the relationship.

For Linda the end of that relationship was a beginning. She knew she would not end up in another destructive marriage. She no longer lived with the illusion that if she were the perfect, submissive wife, her husband would be the perfect husband. Her story does not have a fairy-tale ending, but for the first time in her life, Linda knows that if she finds a growing, changing, Christ-centered man who loves her, then a successful marriage is a possibility!

Chapter 5

Breaking the Cycle of Dysfunction, Codependency, and Addiction

In the past few chapters we've seen how easily people—even those who deeply love God—fall into codependent, compulsive, and addictive behaviors. We've seen how easily families become trapped in dysfunctional relationships and how the harsh realities of dysfunctional family life cause damaged relationships that continue for generations. So where does this knowledge lead us? Are families forever doomed to live this way? Is there any way out of this destructive cycle?

Yes, there is a way out. There is a way to put an end to the craziness. It is possible to handle the intense and diverse emotions of family life and to heal damaged family relationships. But first, let's put the problem into perspective.

We must remember that we live in a fallen world in which nothing is perfect. For some reason we find it easy to say that we live in a fallen world, but we expect our families to be perfect anyway! We must cast aside our unreasonable expectation of family perfection. Every family falls short; every family has some dysfunction—some area of struggle, some degree of pain, some unresolved problems. Thus we all bring some emotional "baggage" into all our relation-ships. This preexisting emotional burden can be a major cause of the difficulties we experience with relationships.

The question, therefore, is not if we sin, but how we sin. The question is not are our families dysfunctional, but in what ways and to what extent are they dysfunctional. The question is not whether we are codependent, but to what degree are we codependent. The question is not do we carry shame, but how much do we limit God's grace by shaming ourselves and others.

We can rejoice because there is hope. The hope of living in this fallen world with all its problems and personal pain is that God doesn't want us to live this way! Codependence is contrary to Christ's commandment to love others as we love ourselves. Jesus did not tell us to love others *more* than we love ourselves; He said *as* we love ourselves. He also has provided us with His personal example of emotional integ-rity in relationships: by speaking that which is honest and true without hidden messages of shame and by maintain-ing His perspective and priorities even when others pressed Him to do otherwise.

When we seek to deal with the sin in our lives and live as if God really matters, He has promised to be with us. We are fallen creatures who need someone greater than ourselves to help us through each day. God is that greater power. He offers His salvation, but that's not all. He is waiting, ready to heal the deep hurts hidden within us. As we identify the painful sources of our emotional and spiritual problems, His healing hand is there to touch and support us. He offers His strength as we deal with our hurts and failures through a lifetime of spiritual growth.

Let's not forget that all families have difficulties and need to learn how to do things differently. We all can, and indeed must, take steps to improve our family lives, our marriages, and the way we feel inside. The sooner we are able to get beyond the need to keep our problems a secret or to pretend that they don't exist, the more quickly healing can occur.

The family is a powerful entity. It can be a formidable

force for destruction or an equally incredible force for healing. Let's look at another family from the Bible that shows the power of the family in promoting either generations of dysfunction or generations of recovery and healing.

Joseph: A Victim of a Dysfunctional Family

Dysfunction in Joseph's family had been brewing for a long time. It began three generations before Joseph was born in the relationship of his great-grandparents, Abraham and Sarah. The story begins in Genesis 12:10, where we learn that a famine caused Abraham to move his family to Egypt. Afraid that his beautiful wife, Sarah, would attract Pharaoh's attention and that Pharaoh would kill him in order to marry her, Abraham pretended that Sarah was his sister. Soon Pharaoh took Sarah into his palace as his wife. He also treated Abraham very well because of her.

Abraham was so interested in his own survival that he cared little about what his deception would mean to Sarah. Years later, Abraham again jeopardized her physical, emotional, and sexual safety by telling another king that she was his sister (Gen. 20:1–18). Scripture tells us little more about their family problems except that bitterness related to Sarah's infertility existed between Sarah and her servant Hagar, who gave birth to Abraham's first son, Ishmael. There is also a record of strife between Sarah's son, Isaac, and Ishmael.

A generation later some of the same destructive behaviors were repeated when, to save himself, Isaac asked his wife, Rebekah, to pretend to be his sister (Gen. 26:7–10). Their twin sons, even before birth, competed against each other (Gen. 25:22–26). Isaac and Rebekah apparently joined in the competition by each choosing a favorite child: Rebekah picked Jacob; Isaac preferred Esau (Gen. 25:28). When Isaac was ill, perhaps ready to die, Rebekah got even with him by helping to deceive him into giving his blessing to Jacob rather than to Esau.

The results of Rebekah's deception were dramatic. Isaac trembled violently (Gen. 27:33). Esau begged bitterly for

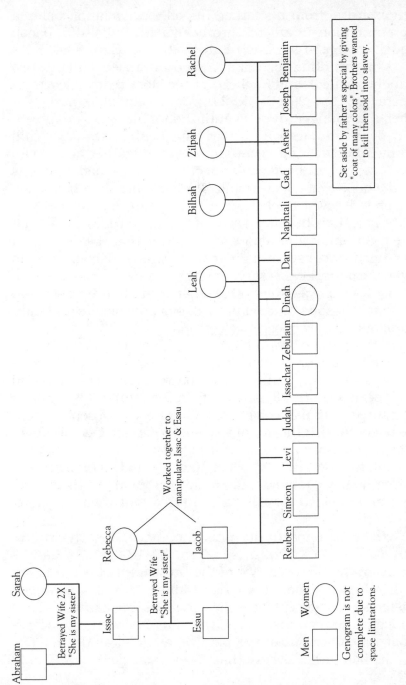

Abraham

Sarah

Betrayed Wife 2X
"She is my sister"

Issac

Betrayed Wife
"She is my sister"

Rebecca

Worked together to
manipulate Issac & Esau

Jacob

Esau

Leah   Bilhah   Zilpah   Rachel

Reuben   Simeon   Levi   Judah   Issachar   Zebulaun   Dinah   Dan   Naphtali   Gad   Asher   Joseph   Benjamin

Set aside by father as special by giving
"coat of many colors". Brothers wanted
to kill then sold into slavery.

Men   Women

Genogram is not
complete due to
space limitations.

© Copyright 1991, Earl R. Henslin

any blessing from his father, his only consolation being a determination to kill his brother (Gen. 27:34–42). Jacob sought refuge in his uncle Laban's house (Gen. 27:43).

While working for Laban, Jacob married Laban's two daughters, Leah and Rachel, but the story reads like a soap opera (see Gen. 29:16—30:24)! Jacob wanted to marry Rachel, the younger, more beautiful daughter. Laban agreed, but deceived Jacob into marrying Leah first. Jacob still wanted Rachel, and eventually he married her also. Leah was deeply hurt by Jacob's rejection, but she had four sons in the hope that Jacob would love her more than her sister. Jacob still loved Rachel more than Leah, but Rachel was bitterly jealous because she was barren and Leah had children. So, in another effort to be better than Leah, Rachel arranged for her servant girl to have sons by Jacob. Then, to even the odds, Leah's servant girl had sons by Jacob! Eventually Rachel was able to have her own children and gave birth to two sons. When it was all over, the sisters and their servants had produced twelve sons.

With this background, is it any wonder that Jacob's sons competed intensely for attention? Lying, resentment, jealousy, favoritism, manipulation, hatred, and deception had long been a "normal" part of life in the family. It isn't much of a surprise that Jacob chose a favorite son, Joseph, whom he honored with the gift of a special robe (see Gen. 37:3–4). The problem was that Joseph's ten older brothers thought the gift to Joseph meant Jacob had rejected all of them. Apparently they could not talk to their father about their problem and decided it was easier to take out their anger on Joseph.

When the opportunity presented itself, Joseph's brothers decided to kill him (see Gen. 37:18–35). As bad as things were, however, two of the brothers, Reuben and Judah, couldn't handle the guilt of killing him and arranged instead to sell Joseph as a slave to a passing caravan. They thought the result would be the same: Joseph, the scapegoat, would be out of the picture, as good as dead. They made their father believe that Joseph was dead, and family life went on.

Meanwhile Joseph, very much alive, began a new life in Egypt (see Gen. 39—41:56). He suffered severe setbacks along the way, but God was clearly with Joseph and greatly blessed him. By interpreting Pharaoh's dreams about seven years of plenty followed by the seven years of famine, Joseph became second in command to Pharaoh. In that position he enjoyed every comfort and luxury Egypt had to offer.

When Joseph's two sons were born, however, we see beyond his successful image and gain insight into his deeper feeling: "Joseph named his firstborn Manasseh and said, 'It is because God has made me forget all my trouble and all my father's household.' The second son he named Ephraim and said, 'It is because God has made me fruitful in the land of my suffering'" (Gen. 41:51–52). Obviously the pain of living in his father's household had deeply troubled Joseph; but these words also reveal his unusual strength and confidence in God's love and provision. God's faithfulness and blessing seemed to have genuinely touched the hurting parts of Joseph's soul—the pain of growing up in a dysfunctional family as well as the suffering he bore as a slave.

Joseph Breaks the Cycle

Everything Joseph told Pharaoh came to pass. The great famine afflicted not only the land of Egypt, but also the land of Canaan, where Joseph's father and brothers lived. The famine was so devastating that apparently his brothers didn't know what to do. Finally Jacob asked them, "Why do you just keep looking at each other? . . . I have heard that there is grain in Egypt. Go down there and buy some for us, so that we may live and not die" (Gen. 42:1–2). Evidently, the loss of Joseph, which had occurred about twenty years earlier, was still a raw wound in the family. Jacob refused to send Benjamin to Egypt with his other sons because he was afraid harm would come to him as it had to Joseph (see Gen. 42:4).

Imagine Joseph's shock as he routinely sold grain to starving people, when he found himself face to face with his brothers (see Gen. 42:7). Imagine the conflicting emotions he must have felt—anger, joy, fear, and relief. I suspect that he didn't quite know what to do, especially since they did not recognize him. So Joseph accused them of being spies and locked them up for three days (see Gen. 42:9–17). Imagine all the schemes Joseph must have entertained during those three days—ways to get even, ways to find out about his father, ways to be united with his family, as well as ways to avoid contact with his brothers. Imagine what his prayers must have been like during those three days.

By the third day, Joseph had devised a plan. Today we would call it a plan for intervention, which is a plan that should cause family members to assume responsibility for their past and present actions and then take positive steps toward changing their dysfunctional ways of relating to each other. So, on the third day, Joseph released his brothers and gave them explicit orders. "If you are honest men, let one of your brothers stay here in prison, while the rest of you go and take grain back for your starving households. But you must bring your youngest brother to me, so that your words may be verified and that you may not die" (Gen. 42:19–20).

The plan started to work. The brothers began talking among themselves about what they had done to Joseph, and they confessed to each other their cruelty. They expressed the fear that their evil deed had caught up with them. Although he hid his feelings from them, their words touched Joseph (see Gen. 42:21–24).

When the brothers returned home, they told Jacob everything that had happened. He was frightened and dismayed at the loss of a second son, who had been left behind in Egypt. However, he so dreaded the possibility of losing Benjamin, too, that he would not allow the brothers to return to Egypt. Only when they again ran out of food did Jacob send his sons, including Benjamin, back to Egypt (see Gen. 41:29—43:14).

Upon their return to Egypt, all eleven of Joseph's brothers joined him in his home for a meal (see Gen. 43:16–34). The sight of his brother Benjamin was more than Joseph could bear; he had to escape to his private room to cry. Imagine the second most powerful person in Egypt—indeed, the world—running into his room to weep. When he regained his composure, Joseph ate with them, filled their sacks with grain, and sent them on their way.

However, Joseph put them through another test to see if their hearts had changed. He had his servants plant his own silver cup in Benjamin's sack of grain, as if it had been stolen. His officers then tracked his brothers down and brought them back to Joseph, as if they were criminals. When Joseph insisted that only Benjamin be imprisoned, Judah begged Joseph to imprison him and let Benjamin go. In his plea, Judah revealed the whole family story—the hidden crime against Joseph, the brothers' concern for their father, and their father's inconsolable sorrow at the loss of Joseph (see Gen. 44).

Scripture then tells us that "Joseph could no longer control himself before all his attendants, and he cried out, 'Have everyone leave my presence!' So there was no one with Joseph when he made himself known to his brothers. And he wept so loudly that the Egyptians heard him, and Pharaoh's household heard about it" (Gen. 45:1–2). What an outpouring of emotion! Given evidence of his brothers' changed hearts, Joseph made himself known to them. He showed his heartfelt forgiveness by saying, "Do not be distressed and do not be angry with yourselves for selling me here, because it was to save lives that God sent me ahead of you" (Gen. 45:5).

God had accomplished a truly marvelous work in Joseph. He had enabled Joseph to forgive the unforgivable. He had worked in Joseph to heal his heart. He had given Joseph the courage to approach his brothers in a way that could bring healing to the family. He had made reconciliation between Joseph and his brothers possible. Genesis 45:14–15 paints a beautiful picture of this process: "Then he threw his arms around his brother Benjamin and wept, and Benjamin embraced him, weeping. And he kissed all his brothers and wept over them. Afterward his brothers talked with him."

As beautiful as this picture is, we have to remember that healing a dysfunctional family is an ongoing process. It doesn't happen all at once. Unless the family is on its guard, it is all too easy to slip back into destructive patterns. I think Joseph recognized this, because when he sent his brothers back to Canaan his parting words were, "Don't quarrel on the way!" (Gen. 45:24).

Families Can Change

Earlier in this book, I shared about some ideas of dysfunction in my own family. I am glad to say that my family has begun to deal with some of those problems. We're certainly not perfect, but we now have an openness we haven't had before and are able to talk about our hurts and share our feelings. We have laid the foundation for healing and now we are able to face the hard truths and realities of life.

I admire my parents' willingness to talk about these issues. They grew up in a time when it was impossible to talk—even with family members—about intimate emotional issues. In the 1950s, when they were in the midst of raising their children, few parenting books were available. In rural Minnesota no one addressed the problems of emotional, physical, or sexual abuse—those problems "happen only in the big cities." Few support groups existed, and those were for alcoholics. Four decades ago, most mothers worked at home. Going to a movie or eating out were rare luxuries. Families often lived in the same neighborhood—not too far from aunts, uncles, and cousins—for generations.

Yet all of this has changed. Today people talk about the most intimate personal matters on national television. Parents have access to a mind-boggling array of child-rearing resources. Abuse is a secret no longer. It is recognized as a problem throughout our society—even in Christian families—and is frequently covered by the news media and graphically portrayed on television. Support groups exist for a seemingly endless list of needs. Today, the majority of women work outside the home. We can see movies nightly on television and, if the evening's choice doesn't suit us, can choose what we prefer at the local video store. For many families, eating out is more common than eating in. Corporate transfers and job changes dictate where families live, and only the most highly motivated families maintain close contact with grandparents, aunts, uncles, and cousins.

These great changes have brought both an increased opportunity and an increased need to change the dysfunctional patterns of our family relationships. The family today is under more stress than ever before. The pressures of society alone can produce confusion, pain, and turmoil—the all too familiar emotions of dysfunctional families—even in the least dysfunctional families. So it is more important than ever that we be able to communicate our positive as well as negative feelings directly, without shame, judgment, defensiveness, or criticism.

The family I was born into forty years ago is different now. The relationship I have with my parents now is different from the one we had twenty years ago. We have begun to admit and talk about our differences. No longer do we blame each other. Each family member has become more open to accepting his or her appropriate responsibility within the family. Shame is being replaced by an ability to accept the legitimacy of each person's perception.

These changes in my family of origin have greatly aided my own healing and recovery. The process of recovery has also made a great difference in my relationships as a husband and father. My relationship with my wife, Karen, is far different from seventeen years ago. My parenting style has changed, too.

Although I have always done the best parenting I knew how to do, my younger children have had the benefit of a more open and less shame-bound relationship than my older children experienced. Even I, a family therapist, must face the painful truth that as my children grow older, I will need to ask their forgiveness and make amends for inadequacies in my parenting. No matter how hard I try, I know I won't be there for them all the time; I know I will unintentionally shame them. In the future I will have to face responsibility for the problems I cause today. When that day comes, I can take encouragement in the fact that I did the best I could.

I am thankful my family is gaining an increased openness and ability to share both painful and happy feelings. We have an empathy and understanding for other family members. We value and respect our own as well as others' ideas, opinions, and feelings. We have confidence that relationships can be close, warm, and nurturing. We have established appropriate spiritual, physical, relational, and emotional boundaries that are based on biblical truth. We have a process for problem resolution so that we can deal with anger in a positive rather than a destructive manner. Our home is becoming an increasingly safe place for our children (and adults!) to develop emotionally, spiritually, and physically and become all that God would have us become.

But these changes in our family did not happen accidently, and they will not happen accidently for you. They are the result of much hard work.

First, we made a deep, careful reflection on our place in the families in which we grew up, a brave and honest look at the dark, sinful sides as well as the good.

Second, we took responsibility for who we are today and determined to do whatever it took to make changes.

Third, we viewed forgiveness as a process of facing feelings of sadness, hurt, grief, and anger.

Fourth, we realized that letting go of the past could happen only after we embraced the emotions of the past.

It's Never Too Late to Change

Perhaps the stories I've shared about David, Solomon, Abigail, Joseph, and myself have touched a deep part of you. Maybe you identified with Absalom as he, in his seemingly rebellious way, vainly tried to right the wrongs done to his sister. Perhaps you, too, have felt Tamar's desolation. Perhaps you're married but, like Abigail, feel as though the total burden of the family rests on your shoulders. Perhaps, as you read about Joseph's interaction with his brothers, you felt an uncontrollable welling up of emotion. Perhaps your compulsiveness and drive to achieve are a bit like Solomon's. Perhaps your family acts a little like mine used to, not really knowing how to handle emotions—even a loving hug.

If so, chances are good that you would benefit by making changes in how you relate to others. Chances are, areas of dysfunction exist in your relationships. Chances are, you exhibit some degree of codependency. Take a look at the following checklist and see if you recognize any of these codependent traits in yourself.

1. Do you find yourself staying in a destructive relationship when circumstances dictate that you should take steps to bring the abuse to an end? (For example, is your spouse having an affair, an alcoholic or drug addict, or emotionally or physically abusive?)

2. Have you ever been hit, grabbed, pinched, pushed, or shoved by someone with whom you are in a close relationship?

3. Do you have trouble saying no when you need to take care of yourself or have too much to do already?

4. When you say no, do you feel guilty?

5. Do you feel that you are the only one holding the marriage or family together?

6. Do you do things for others that they could do for themselves?

7. Do you feel as though you can never do enough for the people with whom you are in relationship?

8. Do you feel love or approval only when you do something for someone else?

9. Do you continually give up or deny your needs and wants?

10. Do you cover up or make excuses for your spouse or someone with whom you are in relationship?

11. Do you feel that you are to blame for most of the problems in your relationships?

12. Do you feel as though you have to be perfect?

13. Do you struggle with compulsive behaviors, such as alcoholism, eating disorders, sexual addiction, workaholism, or drug addiction?

14. Do you feel as though you will never be able to please God?

15. Are you the person who always gets the job done?

16. Do you have trouble setting limits at work or find that you do other people's work for them?

17. Do you usually work later than your coworkers?

18. Do you wish you could be as assertive as people around you?

19. Do you keep your needs and feelings to yourself?

20. Do you ignore symptoms of illness or physical signals that your body needs rest?

If you responded yes to five or more of these questions, you are most likely in a codependent relationship with one or more people. If that's the case, I would strongly encourage you to begin the process of healing and recovery. The process is not easy, but you and those you love have everything to gain!

It is tempting to put off the process of healing and recovery, to think that things aren't that bad or that they will get better tomorrow. But time never heals the hurt of living in a dysfunctional family. The problems never get better on their own. Time only allows the hurt to become more entrenched, the resentment to grow deeper, and daily life to become increasingly difficult. Time heals only if people are actively working toward recovery.

No matter how traumatic a family's dysfunction may be, it's never too late to change. I once counseled a severely depressed man in his early eighties. As he talked, he revealed a life of overwork and overachievement, accompanied by emotional distance and alienation from his children and grandchildren. Slowly and painfully, he realized that he had been excessively critical and overbearing with his children, even emotionally and physically abusive.

In time, memories about his childhood began to surface. Tears rolled down his cheeks when he remembered the times his alcoholic father had physically abused him. When he got in touch with the deep hurt that he had refused to feel for seventy-five years, this man began to move closer emotionally to his adult children. He began to accept responsibility for the damage he had done to them and asked their forgiveness for the ways in which he had abused them. When their feelings of anger, hurt, and resentment were in turn honestly expressed in a healthy way, forgiveness and reconciliation occurred. For the first time in this man's life, a family issue was worked through to a positive resolution!

Because of their father's actions, the man's adult children were able to recognize and change the patterns of emotional abuse by which they were victimizing their children. Generations of abuse were addressed and brought to a halt. Family members began taking risks and revealing their true feelings to one another, bringing about a genuine closeness that none of them had experienced before. All of this happened because a man in his eighties was willing, with God's help, to feel the hurt he had carried inside for seventy-five years and to begin changing how he related to his children. Like Joseph, this man will be able to stand before his Creator knowing that he helped make a positive change in his family.

PART II

Shackled by Shame

Chapter 6

Healthy Shame, Toxic Shame: We'd Better Know the Difference!

An old Jewish proverb says, "Shame is an iron fence that guards us from sin." That's true. Shame convicts us when we do wrong. It is an alarm that goes off when we violate the boundaries God has established. Shame prompts us to repent and make amends. It painfully reminds us of our guilt, thereby encouraging us to avoid the sins that make us feel ashamed. Shame can draw us toward God and forgiveness; this kind of healthy shame is good.

It would be equally true to say, "Shame is an iron fence that keeps us in dysfunction!" This kind of shame communicates far more than guilt; it communicates that we are bad, inferior, and worthless. This kind of shame is destructive to the inner person. Instead of prompting us to deal with our sin, it usually leads us to deny our sin. This kind of shame is not good. It is not healthy. In fact, it can be deadly. We say that this kind of shame is "toxic."

Shame plays a commanding role in our lives. It affects not only our relationship with God, but our relationships with people and our perception of ourselves. Healthy shame helps us maintain functional relationships. Toxic shame, on the other hand, tends to keep us locked in dysfunctional relationships. Since toxic shame plays such a key role in family dysfunction, codependency, and addiction, we would be wise to better understand the phenomenon of shame.

We'll begin our study by exploring the spiritual aspects of shame, then move to the relational. Keep in mind, however, that the different aspects of shame are not independent; they are closely interrelated. When we receive messages of toxic shame on a relational level, for example, we tend to translate those messages into feelings of toxic spiritual shame. Likewise, when we have a healthy concept of spiritual shame we are likely to be less affected by toxic relational shame.

Sin Produces Shame

Shame has been around for a long, long time. It's one of the results of sin. In fact, shame was the immediate emotional response Adam and Eve felt when they bit into the forbidden fruit in the Garden of Eden. Scripture says that as soon as Adam and Eve ate the fruit, "the eyes of both of them were opened, and they realized they were naked; so they sewed fig leaves together and made coverings for themselves" (Gen. 3:7).

No mistake about it, Adam and Eve got the message of shame loud and clear! Before they sinned, Adam and Eve had no guilt and felt no shame. But afterward, surrounded by the pristine beauty of the Garden of Eden, the guilt of their sin became glaringly evident to them. They were ashamed of themselves and were convicted of their sin. The shame they felt at that time was healthy spiritual shame. It let them know that they had done something dreadfully wrong and needed to take steps to correct their error.

Guilt stems from the violation or transgression of God's principles of living as expressed in Scripture (for example, adultery equals sin). Guilt can, therefore, be handled cognitively. Healthy shame is the feeling of having violated that code and is a feeling that has to be taken care of emotionally. It is a feeling that can help motivate us to ask God for forgiveness, take steps to ask forgiveness from the person we have sinned against, and if possible, take the steps to make amends with those we have hurt or sinned against.

It isn't easy to follow the promptings of healthy shame and take steps that will bring forgiveness and healing. Most of us will do anything—indeed everything—we can think of to avoid facing our sin and its consequences. We will rationalize, blame others, and even deny our actions. We will go to great lengths to avoid saying the words, "I'm sorry," or "Lord, I have sinned." Self-honesty is not easy, but it is necessary. When we refuse to deal properly with healthy shame and the reality of our sin, we find ourselves at a spiritual impasse, unable to ask for forgiveness and pursue a healthy relationship with God.

That is what happened to Adam and Eve. Instead of dealing with their sin, they tried to hide it. First, they covered themselves to escape the shame of their mutual nakedness. Then, to their horror, they heard God approaching! In desperation, they tried to hide from Him (see Gen. 3:8). They did not want to face God and confess what they had done, so they put as much distance between themselves and God as possible.

Their decision had devastating spiritual consequences for themselves and the rest of the human race. Adam and Eve were cast out of the Garden of Eden and lived the rest of their lives in shame, in perpetual need of atonement for their sins. Without the reality of God's grace and forgiveness, their lives became an ongoing struggle with toxic shame.

The same is true for us. Just like Adam and Eve, we feel shame when we sin. The only way to escape the shackles of toxic shame is to face our sin and deal with it properly, in the way God requires.

A Proper Response to Shame

Once we become aware of our sin in contrast to God's holiness, we inevitably feel shame. It is a natural result of being in the presence of a holy God. It helps us realize that we are fatally flawed and need a Savior who can reestablish our relationship with God. If our response to God is one of humility, a realization that we are sinners in need of His forgiveness and mercy, then shame has accomplished its purpose. We can then receive God's forgiveness and healing. If, on the other hand, we do not deal with healthy shame according to God's standard of repentance, then it becomes a toxic force that leads us down an increasingly destructive path.

Adam and Eve chose the wrong response to shame; they chose the path of destruction, the way of toxic shame. However, Scripture tells us about another man, the prophet Isaiah, who also found himself overwhelmed by shame while in the presence of God. Unlike Adam and Eve, Isaiah did not hide. With deep fear, he confessed his sin:

> *I saw the Lord seated on a throne, high and exalted, and the train of his robe filled the temple. Above him were seraphs. . . . And they were calling to one another:*
>
> > *"Holy, holy, holy is the LORD Almighty;*
> > *the whole earth is full of his glory."*
>
> *At the sound of their voices the doorposts and thresholds shook and the temple was filled with smoke.*
> *"Woe to me!" I cried. "I am ruined! For I am a man of unclean lips, and I live among a people of unclean lips, and my eyes have seen the King, the LORD Almighty."*
> *Then one of the seraphs flew to me with a live coal in his hand, which he had taken with tongs from the altar. With it he touched my mouth and said, "See, this has touched your lips; your guilt is taken away and your sin atoned for."*
> *Then I heard the voice of the LORD. . . . (Isa. 6:1–8)*

In God's presence, Isaiah was overwhelmed by the reality of his sinfulness. He felt his impurity so intensely that he cried out, "I am ruined!" That is how healthy shame makes us feel. Yet, because Isaiah was repentant, God purified him, which enabled him to go into God's presence.

God Is Not a Shaming Ogre!

God's immediate response to Isaiah's overwhelming awareness of his sin teaches us an important lesson about God and shame. God is not a shaming ogre who wants us to squirm in perpetual horror of our sin. He does not want us to live under the unbearable weight of shame. He is a holy God who cannot stand sin but is also a loving, forgiving God. He is always ready to accept our confessions of guilt and to purify us, releasing us from the bonds of shame.

In Old Testament times, God's people sacrificed animals as peace offerings to Him, as atonement for sin, as a way to escape the imprisonment of toxic shame. We clearly see the extent of Israel's sin and shame when Solomon finished building the Lord's temple. When the nation of Israel prepared to bring the Ark of the Covenant into the temple, they sacrificed "so many sheep and cattle that they could not be recorded or counted" (1 Kings 8:5). Later, when Solomon dedicated the temple, he sacrificed 22,000 cattle and 120,000 sheep and goats in order to demonstrate the nation of Israel's repentance and make them worthy before God (see 1 Kings 8:63). Apparently Israel had a tremendous amount of sin and shame to unload!

God fully accepted their sacrifice. In fact, when the priests brought the Ark into the temple, the cloud representing the glory of God filled the temple. The cloud of God's presence so overwhelmed the temple that the priests had to leave—they couldn't even perform their duties (see 1 Kings 8:10–11)! This certainly isn't the image of a God who wants His people to remain in shame. He offers full release from shame to those who repent.

We see the same image of God in the New Testament. Jesus was sent as the ultimate sacrifice, the ultimate release from sin and its debilitating shame. In Jesus' dealings with people on earth, we see a remarkable absence of toxic shame. Although the religious structures of the day were extremely legalistic and shame oriented, with religious leaders almost gloating in the power they had to shame God's people, Jesus took no pleasure in shaming others. Rather, He proclaimed God's truth and way of repentance. When His message was accepted, He offered forgiveness.

We see a profound absence of toxic shame in Jesus' interaction with the Samaritan woman at the well. On the basis of cultural, religious, and spiritual norms, Jesus had ample opportunity to shame this woman. At that time, women were looked down upon and did not share equal social and intellectual status with men. So it was highly unusual for a man to strike up a conversation in public with a woman he did not know. Jews also considered Samaritans to be an inferior race and would not even associate with them.

Jesus, however, directed no shame at her for being a woman or a Samaritan. Furthermore, even though He was the Son of God and had every right to shame her for her adultery, He did not do so. Neither did He condemn her. Instead, in a matter-of-fact manner, He pointed out her sin. When she responded truthfully and expressed her desire for living water, Jesus did not dwell on her sin. Instead, He focused on meeting the true need of her spiritual condition.

This is the nature of healthy shame that comes from God. It makes us aware—even painfully aware—of our sin and unworthiness. Yet God never leaves us hopelessly in shame. He always offers a way of repentance, forgiveness, and healing—a way of living without shame.

Dealing with Other Messages of Shame

Unfortunately, healthy spiritual shame is only a part of the shame picture. Other types of shame have an equally significant impact on our lives. For instance, as people who live in a fallen world, we may experience toxic spiritual shame—a dark distortion of healthy shame. As sinful people who live in relationship with other sinful people, we may experience relational shame. Like spiritual shame, relational shame can be either healthy or toxic. The diagram on page 81 illustrates the types of shame we can experience and their primary effects.

Isaiah's actions when he was in God's presence illustrate

Healthy Spiritual Shame

- Convicts us of Sin
- Prompts us to Repent
- Draws us toward God

Healthy Relational Shame

- Enables us to say "I'm Sorry" when we have injured others
- Helps us set boundries, such as modesty, privacy
- Healthy Embarrassment

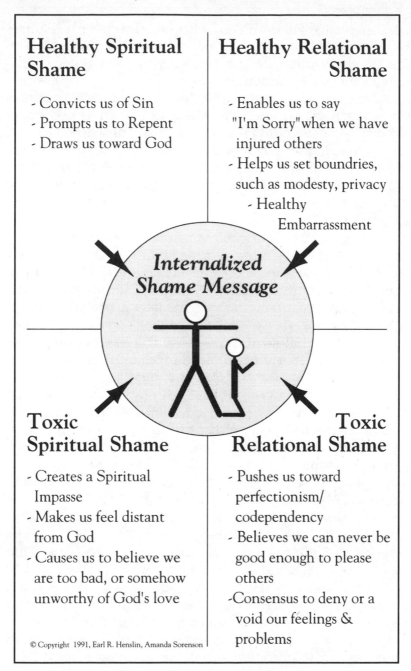

Internalized Shame Message

Toxic Spiritual Shame

- Creates a Spiritual Impasse
- Makes us feel distant from God
- Causes us to believe we are too bad, or somehow unworthy of God's love

© Copyright 1991, Earl R. Henslin, Amanda Sorenson

Toxic Relational Shame

- Pushes us toward perfectionism/ codependency
- Believes we can never be good enough to please others
- Consensus to deny or a void our feelings & problems

- Depending upon the shame messages we receive & our ability to set boundries, our internalized shame message may fall anywhere on this chart

what happens when we deal with healthy spiritual shame. He was convicted of his sin before God. He desired repentance, and through God's forgiveness he was able to establish an intimate relationship with God.

Adam and Eve, on the other hand, suffered the effects of toxic spiritual shame. They did not heed the voice of healthy shame and deal with their sin properly. Instead, they refused to take responsibility for their actions. By doing so, they moved into a state of chronic toxic shame, which caused them to feel profoundly unworthy and bad about themselves and created an impasse in their relationship with God.

Just as healthy spiritual shame lets us know when we have violated God's laws, so also healthy relational shame lets us know when we need to make amends to another person we have injured. Healthy relational shame also helps us know where to set boundaries to protect ourselves, such as boundaries of modesty, boundaries that determine the level of intimacy we allow in our relationships, and boundaries that enable us to say no to inappropriate demands on our time or physical person. Healthy relational shame also makes us feel uncomfortable when our protective boundaries are threatened or violated. However, when we don't deal with the messages of healthy relational shame properly, we fall victim to toxic shame.

For example, when we don't make amends for the wrongs we do to others, we continue to feel bad about our actions. This feeling usually turns into a bad feeling about ourselves, which is toxic relational shame. When we allow others to violate our boundaries, we also feel as if there is something bad, wrong, or inferior about ourselves. This, too, is toxic relational shame. However, unresolved healthy relational shame is not the only source of toxic relational shame. As we will see later, deep feelings of toxic shame also occur when we grow up in a dysfunctional family.

As we grow up and go through life, all of us receive many messages of shame, which can be toxic or healthy, relational or spiritual. After repeated or intense exposure to shame messages, we internalize them, which means we learn to accept them as being true. John Bradshaw describes this process well: "The most destructive aspect of shame is the process whereby shame moves from being a feeling to being a state of being."[1] Once we internalize a shame message, we make conclusions about ourselves based on that message. The effect can be devastating.

Depending on which types of shame messages we receive and our ability to set protective boundaries, our internalized shame messages may fall anywhere on the shame diagram. David, for example, internalized mostly healthy spiritual shame messages. However, the relational shame messages he internalized were primarily toxic. Other people may internalize many toxic spiritual and relational shame messages, while internalizing very few healthy shame messages. When we internalize toxic shame messages, we are inclined to adopt dysfunctional, codependent, compulsive, and addictive behaviors in a vain attempt to anesthetize the bad feelings of toxic shame. People in recovery are actively working to internalize healthy shame messages and let go of the toxic shame messages that have kept them in dysfunction.

Toxic Shame: The Number-one Message Of Dysfunctional Families

Children who grow up in dysfunctional families receive messages of toxic shame on a daily basis. Because they are children, they have normal needs and desires to be held, to be emotionally nurtured, to be given the opportunity to explore and ask questions, and to be allowed to test boundaries and establish their own identities. Yet these needs often are unmet in dysfunctional families. Worse, children in dysfunctional families often receive punishment or shame because they have these needs.

Unfortunately, children develop their feelings about themselves according to the way their parents respond to their needs. When their needs are unmet or shamed, children feel that they are bad or have done something wrong to cause the negative response. The tragedy is that these feel-

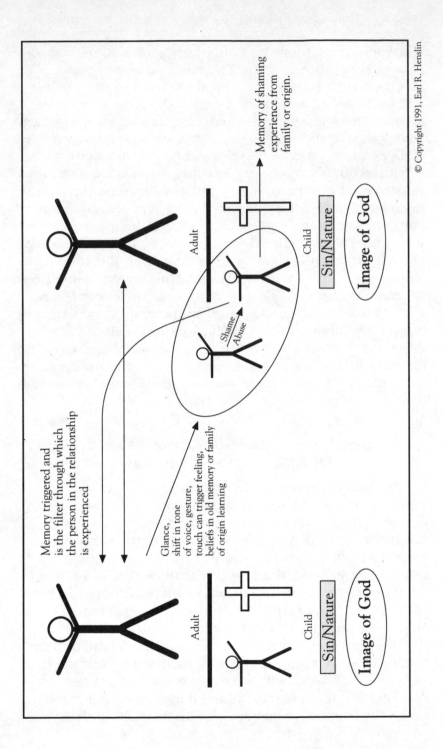

Memory triggered and is the filter through which the person in the relationship is experienced

Glance, shift in tone of voice, gesture, touch can trigger feeling, beliefs in old memory or family of origin learning

Adult

Child

Sin/Nature

Image of God

Shame
Abuse

Adult

Child

Sin/Nature

Image of God

Memory of shaming experience from family or origin.

ings of toxic relational shame aren't just felt and forgotten; they are stored in the unconscious.

The diagram of the person shows the memories, shame, and feelings that a child internalizes, or stores in the unconscious. The block between the conscious and the unconscious represents all of the things we do to keep ourselves from feeling the effects of what is stored in the unconscious.

Children naturally do not know how to deal with feelings of shame; it is something they need to learn how to do. But when shame dominates their environment, they have no safe place or relationship through which to deal with those feelings. So they internalize the toxic shame messages in the unconscious, where those messages continue to have an impact on their lives. Thus it is common for children from dysfunctional families to feel worthless, to feel bad about themselves at the core of their being, and to carry those feelings into adulthood. Barb's story is a good example of how children internalize shame simply by growing up in dysfunctional families.

Barb's father died when she was only five years old. Her mother, an alcoholic, remarried a successful attorney who was highly respected in the church and the community. Only Barb and her mother knew that he, too, was an alcoholic. When he drank, he was loud, controlling, abusive, and shaming.

Every evening, when Barb heard his car pull into the driveway, her body clicked into a state of tension and hyperalertness. As soon as her stepfather entered the house, Barb's home was no longer a safe place to be. Her stepfather and mother would usually get drunk and start screaming at each other. Most nights, her stepfather would hit Barb and call her names. As she approached adolescence, he added another weapon of shame to his nightly arsenal: he would make sexual comments about her. Because Barb's mother was also drunk, she was in no position to protect her daughter from his shame and abuse.

Children who grow up in situations like this suffer from toxic shame. It is shaming for children to live in emotionally dangerous homes. It is shaming for children to see their parents fight. It is shaming for children to be hit or verbally abused by their parents. It is shaming for parents to violate their children's sexual boundaries. It is shaming when parents are emotionally unavailable to protect or care for their children. All of these shaming messages make children feel defective, inadequate, bad, and worthless.

Barb felt shamed as a child and as an adult. When she came to me, she struggled with deep depression. She was also overly sensitive to the noise level in her home. A rise in the noise level or a change in a family member's tone of voice would trigger deep feelings of extreme anger, fear, and shame. Not knowing the source of these emotions, Barb would then heap additional shame upon herself for having such "bad" feelings. In her confused state of toxic shame, Barb even felt that she was a bad Christian because she had those feelings!

The Power of Toxic Shame

When we internalize messages of toxic shame, our sense of worthlessness affects every relationship we have. It affects our relationships with our parents, spouses, siblings, and children. It affects our relationships with our coworkers and teachers. It affects our interaction with the trash collector, other drivers on the road, and even the checker at the grocery store!

Normal, daily interactions with people trigger the deep feelings of toxic shame that reside within us. Once the shame feelings have been triggered, we move into a cycle of shame in which we lock on to a particular behavior to protect ourselves from further shaming. We may defend ourselves, argue, or withdraw from others.

All of these protective behaviors perpetuate the shame cycle. They prevent us from taking steps to clearly identify the shame issues, to place responsibility for the shame where it belongs, and to move toward forgiveness and healing. Rodney Clapp aptly describes the effects of toxic shame:

> The irony of shame is that hiding and covering our vulner-
> ability only increases it. . . . Life for ashamed people who
> cannot admit shame is a complicated and tense affair. Yet,
> unable to admit and deal with their shame, such people
> can only use shame to try to stay one step ahead. Shame
> fuels pecking orders and status symbols.[2]

The perfectionistic standard that a shame-bound person must adhere to in order to feel worthwhile is devastating. If we are bound by shame, we not only apply that standard of perfection to ourselves but use it to gauge the worthiness of others with whom we are in relationship. We leave others with the feeling that no matter what they do, they will never be good enough for us. We require a history of perfection before we begin to let go of the hurt or anger that others have caused us. For all practical purposes, forgiveness is nonexistent because those who want our forgiveness have to prove their worthiness.

It is very threatening to offer forgiveness to another, to grant a measure of goodness, when we feel so bad inside that we have to prove that we are better than others. Toxic shame doesn't want to offer forgiveness; it wants to receive justice! Toxic shame creates a need for others to pay for the wrong they have done; it wants the offender to suffer and crawl! Toxic shame isn't satisfied with an eye for an eye; it wants the arms and legs as well! Toxic shame wants ven-geance, and it certainly doesn't want to relinquish venge-ance to the Lord (see Rom. 12:19)!

Toxic shame makes it difficult to request and accept for-giveness because it makes us feel even more unworthy if we dare to admit our faults. When we have wronged another, toxic shame makes us want to cry out, "I'm right! I'm right!" How can we say, "Forgive me," or "I'm sorry" when saying those words leaves us feeling as if we're even worse people? If taking responsibility for our actions or placing appropriate responsibility on another makes us feel even more shame, we naturally will defend with all our might whatever self-righteousness or goodness we can muster.

Locked up in the face-saving cycle of toxic shame, some

of us may survive through massive denial that, in reality, only propels us toward codependency, perfectionism, compulsive behaviors, and even addiction. Many of us feel that we must shoulder all of the responsibility for what happens in our relationships. We feel we are so bad and unworthy that it simply isn't possible for anyone else to bear any relational responsibility. The problem is that when we assume total responsibility for the relationship, others are free to hurt us over and over again, which only fuels the fires of shame and dysfunction.

Most debilitating of all, toxic shame affects our relationship with God. It is nearly impossible for shame-bound individuals to feel God's grace. When we internalize toxic relational shame messages, we tend to feel spiritually unlovable and unredeemable. In that state of shame, we cannot feel God's forgiveness. It doesn't sink in because we believe we are unworthy of forgiveness—from God or anyone else. It's as if we walk around waiting for someone to dole out sufficient extreme punishment so that perhaps we can begin to prove that we are worthy of forgiveness. Although God's grace says, "You are forgiven because of what Christ has done," we really don't feel loved or forgiven. Most of us cannot truly feel God's healing grace or begin to offer it to others until we have dealt with some of the toxic shame issues we carry inside.

Are you beginning to see the tremendous role that toxic shame plays in our lives? It certainly is a far cry from the pure feelings of guilt that God intended us to feel and respond to, isn't it? In the next few chapters, we'll take a closer look at the insidious phenomenon of toxic shame that keeps us locked into dysfunction and codependency.

Chapter 7

The Family:
Spawning Ground for Shame

God designed the family to be the nurturing unit that enables children to grow up and go out into the world with the ability to express His goodness in all of life. Thus the family has tremendous potential to affirm and build up its members from one generation to the next. Parents, grandparents, siblings, aunts, uncles, and cousins each play a unique role in this nurturing and growth process.

My grandmother, for example, was a beautifully warm and nurturing person. She graduated from college in the early 1900s, when few women did so. She then taught in a country school and later became a farmer's wife. Throughout her life she maintained interest in a variety of subjects and read broadly. Her quiet, strong faith expressed God's love to those who were close to her. When she spoke, you could feel a wisdom that had been born out of life's tough times. It just felt good to be around her—not only for me, but for the other farm kids who stopped in to visit her. A woman with a heart of gold, she filled a need that only a grandmother could fill.

Her expression of warmth and caring illustrates the way God intended the normal needs of growing children to be met within the family. But in a dysfunctional family, these needs are met in less than positive ways. A child's need for a grandparent may be met with disinterest or criticism. Parents may relinquish to others their unique ability to teach their children how to set boundaries and work out conflicts. Children may also be required to fulfill parental duties. When the family isn't the nurturing unit God intends it to be, the result is devastating.

Setting Boundaries—the Family's Biggest Job

In dysfunctional, rather than nurturing, families, children grow up under the curse of toxic shame. Their needs are not met, and dysfunction seems normal to them. As a result, they grow up with confused, damaged, or even nonexistent boundaries. Let's take a closer look at boundaries so we can better understand the role they play in toxic shame and family dysfunction.

Boundaries are the beliefs and feelings that serve as invisible fences to protect us—spiritually, emotionally, and physically. One way to illustrate a boundary is to think of it in terms of a house. A house keeps us safe from strangers, animals, trucks, or anything else that might come in. A house keeps us dry, protecting us from the rain. It keeps us warm in winter, protecting us from the chilling winds, and cool in summer, sheltering us from the sun's burning rays. A house provides a safe place to live. It is a physical boundary that we can see and touch.

We all have physical boundaries that keep us safe. We are keenly aware of the boundary of our visible, physical bodies, but we are usually less aware of our invisible physical boundaries. Although we can't see the invisible boundaries, we can certainly feel them. The following exercise will enable you to feel an invisible physical boundary.

Stand up and ask a friend or family member to walk toward you. At some point as the person approaches you, you will begin to feel uncomfortable. That point of discomfort represents your physical boundary with that person. Your boundary may be anywhere from a few inches to several feet away from you. If your boundaries are severely damaged, you might begin to feel uncomfortable when the person is on the other side of the room, or you might allow the person to walk right into you!

One of the most important tasks for parents to accomplish is to help children establish protective boundaries. Children come into the world without boundaries. They are helpless and need complete protection and safety. Parents provide that protection and safety for their children during infancy. As children grow up, however, parents need to teach them how to set boundaries so the children will continue to be appropriately protected throughout life. Some of the boundaries parents must establish include:

• Setting firm limits and intervening if the children move into something that is harmful or potentially destructive. (This type of boundary setting is especially important in adolescence and is often greeted with unhappiness.)

• Stepping in to stop shaming or abusive behavior that others (including extended family members) may inflict.

• Respecting their children's need for privacy and modesty.

• Protecting their children from pornography and other inappropriate sexual messages that may appear on television or in books and magazines.

• Respecting the manner in which their children connect with God.

• Helping children learn what their appropriate responsibilities are (and are not) in various kinds of relationships.

• Defining appropriate behavior in different situations.

• Teaching children that no one needs to touch their bodies or private areas, and that it is okay to say no when physical closeness makes them feel uncomfortable.

As you can see, boundaries are necessary to ensure our personal safety. When parents set spiritual, emotional, and physical boundaries, children are safe and have the opportunity to learn, express creativity, and grow. Parents must set boundaries for young children because children aren't able to set their own boundaries until early adolescence. If a child's boundaries are violated or damaged during early childhood, that child will have difficulty setting boundaries as an adolescent and often as an adult.

Rather than teaching their children how to establish appropriate boundaries, parents of dysfunctional families fail to teach boundaries and often violate boundaries. Emotional, spiritual, and physical boundaries that parents of dysfunctional families often violate include:

• Raging at their children.
• Ignoring or scorning their children's feelings.
• Touching their children sexually, making inappropriate sexual comments, or viewing pornography with their children.
• Turning to their children, rather than to their spouses, for emotional support.
• Physically abusing their children (including excessive physical discipline, such as slapping a child in the face).

When boundaries are violated, even if the child doesn't know that boundaries are supposed to exist, a child feels the wounds deep inside. The very spirit of the child is wounded and shamed, so the child internalizes horrible feelings of worthlessness and inadequacy. That shame leaves tremendous holes in the child's self-concept and lays the groundwork for codependency, compulsive behavior, and perfectionism.

The Role of Shame in David's Family

Once we understand how important boundaries are, it's easy to see how toxic shame can become the dominant force in a dysfunctional family, dictating how the family operates and how its members relate to one another. We've already explored the dysfunctional nature of David's family. Now let's examine David's family tree from a slightly different perspective to see how shame governs interaction between members of dysfunctional families. I'm sure you will recognize the toxic shame messages and boundary violations!

Individuals in shame-bound families tend to place the blame for their difficulties on other family members, not on themselves.   Amnon, for example, felt shame because of what he had done to Tamar. Instead of repenting and making amends, however, he rejected her. In so doing, he blamed her for his sin and successfully shifted the emotional burden of his shame onto Tamar (see 2 Sam. 13:15). Tragically, other family members (with the exception of Absalom) made no attempt to direct the shame back to Amnon, where it belonged.

In shame-based families today, a husband may blame his affair on his wife's lack of sexual responsiveness. Rather than taking responsibility for his actions, he tries to make his wife carry his shame. If the wife has good boundaries, he won't be able to do this successfully.

In shame-based families, feelings are considered to be "bad," so emotions are ignored, denied, or punished. Amnon shamed Tamar not only by raping her, but also by ignoring her feelings and pleas. Tamar's only recourse was to express her feelings openly and mourn her loss, which she did by crying and putting ashes on her head.

Tamar's legitimate emotional response, however, only produced greater shame for her. Absalom, who knew that she had been violated, told her to keep quiet. When he spoke those words, her heart was irrevocably broken; the brother who truly cared for her denied her permission to feel or express any emotion. He viewed Tamar's emotions only as an embarrassment to the family.

In light of this treatment, it isn't surprising that Tamar lived the remainder of her life as a "desolate woman." She had experienced the shaming humiliation of incestuous rape, and her father and brothers had further shamed her by rejecting her emotional response to the rape. Her entire family had shamed her by continuing to live as if nothing had happened. With these three strikes against her, it's no wonder that Tamar suffered from insurmountable feelings of shame and unworthiness for the rest of her life.

In a similar way, adults today feel a greater or lesser degree of shame because of the way in which their families of origin handled emotions. For instance, shame is often communicated by merely a look or a glance. A child who wants to share about a particular hurt inside may approach a parent, but if the parent is busy reading or watching television and doesn't want to be disturbed, the child's approach may be greeted with a frown. The child then interprets the frown as anger and rejection and feels shame. When the child feels shame, he or she won't share the hurt but will shove the hurt and shame deep inside, where they do their dirty work on the child's self-concept.

Certain members of shame-based families tend to dominate and strive to maintain the status quo. Families who live in shame also live in fear of change. This fear makes the families emotionally fragile. The least upset can cause tremendous upheaval because the important issues have never been dealt with properly. Years after Tamar was raped, for example, we see an ongoing power struggle—which is very much a struggle for change—between David and Absalom.

When Absalom first tried to bring about change by bringing the family together two years after Amnon raped Tamar, David resisted the change. David, who just wanted the problem to go away, perceived anything that threatened to resurrect the problem as a threat to the family peace (such as it was). Although he refused to exercise his proper responsibility as king and father, David tried to control circumstances and maintain the status quo by keeping certain family members apart. However, when the appropriate family member doesn't assume proper authority, another individual will assume that authority to the detriment of that individual and the entire family. For the remainder of Absalom's life, he and David struggled for control of the family, and even the kingdom.

Fossum and Mason, in their book *Facing Shame*, describe the shame-based family as being excessively controlling:

> Commonly, the control principle is motivated not so much by a drive to power as by a drive for predictability and safety. Beneath the power-oriented, manipulative behavior we usually see a frightened person. . . . Given the fundamental unpredictability and insecurity of life, when the system is organized around controlling what cannot be controlled, many failures, stresses and distortions of human experience are the side effects.[1]

I frequently see control and change issues at work in the shame-based families I counsel. For example, a family member may call me between sessions to let me know the "real problems" in the family, hoping to maintain control of the counseling process. Invariably, those problems bolster the caller's righteousness and shame other family members. In other families, the parents may try to control every aspect of their children's lives long after the children are capable of handling things on their own. One teenager's parents, for example, didn't allow her to decide what clothes to wear to school each day!

Shaming responses that communicate the worthlessness of specific individuals are common in shame-based families.   Perhaps the clearest, most devastating shaming response is that of silence. Tamar certainly experienced it; so did Absalom during his years of exile, when he was not allowed into David's presence. Such silence communicates volumes of negative, destructive feedback: "You are bad! You should be ashamed of yourself! You should have known better! You are not worth my time or effort!" A refusal to communicate allows emotional wounds to fester, often to the point at which irrevocable damage occurs.

David's lack of response to Tamar was shaming. If he had held Amnon accountable for what he had done, Tamar's self-respect would have been restored. She would have again felt worthy to be the king's daughter. A similar shaming occurs when a parent silently observes the abuse of his or her children at the hands of the other parent. To preserve the child's feelings of self-worth, the nonabusive parent must step in and stop the abuse.

The Dreadful Shame of Family Abandonment

Like shame, abandonment is one of the deepest, most devastating feelings a child can experience. Abandonment can be a feeling of being all alone, a feeling that absolutely no one loves you or cares about you, or a feeling that you could disappear and no one would notice that you were gone. These are extremely painful—even terrifying— feelings for children to experience. In adulthood, these dreadful feelings usually stay in the unconscious self, but they are easily triggered by daily experiences and are often expressed in disguise—through such emotions as anger, anxiety, defensiveness, or neediness.

Feelings of abandonment can stem from a variety of sources and childhood experiences. For example, children whose parents divorce often suffer from feelings of abandonment. These children often feel that they did something bad to cause the divorce. Also, it isn't uncommon for young children to have minimal contact with their noncustodial parent following a divorce. In some cases, children may see the noncustodial parent only one or two times during the remainder of their growing-up years or may never see that parent again. Even children who frequently visit their noncustodial parent may feel abandoned, especially if the parent remarries.

Feelings of abandonment aren't limited to children of absentee parents. Parents can be physically present, but emotionally disconnected from life and their children. A parent with a compulsive disease, for example, may provide food and shelter but be incapable of providing appropriate emotional attachment and support. In fact, this type of emotional abandonment is even more damaging than physical abandonment.

Physical and emotional abandonment often go hand in hand when a parent has a compulsive disease. When the parent is involved in the compulsive disease, he or she may be physically as well as emotionally absent. Obviously, a chemically addicted parent is emotionally unavailable much of the time. If the addiction causes lapses in consciousness, the parent becomes physically unavailable as well. A parent who is addicted to work is emotionally and intellectually preoccupied with work and becomes physically absent while at the workplace. In some instances of sexual addiction, the parent's compulsive affairs produce emotional and physical abandonment.

These are not the only situations that produce feelings of abandonment. Children may feel abandoned when a parent dies, perhaps even feeling responsible for the parent's death. Our mobile culture, which forces families to frequently pull up roots and leave the security of familiar communities, churches, neighborhoods, and schools, may contribute to feelings of abandonment. Adopted children may feel abandoned by their birth parents. Children who attend boarding schools far away from home, such as missionary children, may also feel abandoned. Children who suffer trauma, particularly at the hands of their parents, may feel isolated and desperately alone.

Regardless of the cause, the tragic result of parental abandonment is always the same: The child invariably carries the blame and shame for the abandonment. When abandonment occurs, the child internalizes the shame and truly believes that something he or she did or did not do caused the abandonment. The child feels that he or she wasn't good enough to please the parent(s) and thereby avoid the abandonment. The toxic shame the child feels isn't far from the truth, because in many cases the parent is, in effect, saying that the child or family is less worthy of attention than other relationships, whether they be with people, food, sex, work, or even Christian ministry.

Children carry the shame of abandonment into adult life, where it can have a frightening impact. One woman I counseled was a strong, capable executive who was unable to set good boundaries in her personal life. She had a strong dependence on men and repeatedly found herself in abusive relationships. When she was a child, she was adopted into an alcoholic family and was sexually abused by an older brother.

Although we had worked through many of the alcoholic and sexual abuse issues, she was still unable to get a handle on her personal relationships with men. As it turned out, she suffered from strong feelings of abandonment with which she had never before connected. An undeniable, inner part of this woman wondered why her birth mother didn't want her and felt that she wasn't as good as everybody else.

When she identified her feelings of abandonment, she proceeded to search for her birth family. Although her birth mother had been dead for several years when she began her search, the woman was able to contact an uncle and ask him about her birth family. Her uncle was thrilled to hear from her. "I've been praying for years that I would be able to talk to you," he said. "I feel so bad that you were adopted out of our family. I wanted to keep you. I was there when you were born. I held you. I loved you then, and I've felt bad for all this time!"

The uncle then told her that her mother, who was married and had two teenaged children, had had an affair and gotten pregnant. Theirs was a religious family, and the shame was so great that the mother sent the two older children to boarding school and went into hiding until after the baby was born. Only the uncle and an aunt had contact with the mother during that time. Afterward, life went on as if nothing had happened. In fact, the older children knew nothing about their younger half-sister until just before their mother died.

The woman then contacted her half-brother and half-sister and was welcomed by both of them. As she got in touch with her past, her feelings of abandonment began to dissipate. She was finally able to set good limits in her relationships with men.

What Shame Teaches Children About Life

The shame of growing up in a dysfunctional family and the shame of abandonment leave a child with strong feelings of unworthiness. These feelings may cause the child to feel unworthy of being in relationships or of making good choices in relationships (as in the case of the woman described above). They may cause a child to feel unworthy of educational or vocational accomplishment and lead to failure in school or on the job. Unfortunately, it takes very little negative input to produce strong feelings of toxic shame.

Feelings of toxic shame obviously occur when a child is physically or sexually abused within the family. But feelings of shame can result from far less severe—even seemingly insignificant—incidents. For instance, a child will be shamed when a parent overreacts to a spilled glass of milk. Shame also occurs when a child approaches a parent, but is rebuffed or ignored. The child will then devise an explanation for the parent's behavior. Usually the child concludes, *I'm not good enough. I did something wrong.*

When a child begins to accumulate these messages of toxic shame, everything he or she does is affected. A family environment in which shame or abandonment plays a dominant role teaches a child to live by the following rules:[2]

Be in control of all behavior and interaction with others. That way no one can shame you.

Always be "right" and do the "right" thing. There's no difference between bad behavior and a bad person, so in order not to be bad, be perfect.

If things don't go right, blame someone else. That way you're always better than the people around you.

Deny feelings, especially negative or vulnerable ones like anxiety, fear, loneliness, grief, or rejection. Those feelings can get out of hand, but if you don't have them, you're safe. You know you won't experience something you can't handle.

Don't expect reliability or constancy in relationships. Since people are unreliable, it's much safer to be attached to things like food, alcohol, sex, work, or money.

When children from dysfunctional families grow up and continue to live by these and other toxic, self-protecting rules, they are robbed of the joy of life. They usually find it extremely difficult to accept from others expressions of love, care, approval, praise, or other positive emotions. It's almost as if a child from a dysfunctional family carries a hurt, shamed little boy or girl inside who feels so unworthy that he or she is compelled to discount any positive expression of emotion from others. These children then feel that nothing they do will ever be good enough. They are haunted by the fear that, *if they only knew what I was really like, they wouldn't love me.*

It is also very difficult for adults who grew up in shame-based families to feel any joy or happiness in their accomplishments. For example, a shamed adult may finish a major project at work and be highly praised for it, but will feel no real joy in either the accomplishment or the praise. Instead, that adult will be so caught up in proving his or her worth that he or she will plunge right in to the next project without ever experiencing the good feelings of accomplishment or achievement. A pat on the back or a hug of appreciation doesn't go any deeper than the person's clothes. All the appreciation stays outside; it doesn't sink down and touch the hurting boy or girl inside.

Who knows how many songs have never been sung, how many pictures have never been drawn, or how many poems have never been written because toxic shame said, "It's not good enough!" Who knows how many playful games, creative ideas, or romantic moments never came to fruition because toxic shame said, "You'll be laughed at—again!" Who knows how many joyful shouts and winning smiles never happened because toxic shame said, "This isn't really success, but the next thing might be!"

How Shame Sabotages Our Relationships

In addition to providing very limited rules for living, toxic shame tends to make us very defensive. After all, we have to be right or perfect in order to protect ourselves from further shame. From a shame-bound perspective, any failure or lack of perfection proves our unworthiness. Such an overwhelming feeling of worthlessness is an unbearable burden that leads to overreaction and defensiveness.

I have had to deal with these feelings and responses in my own life. Many of my childhood experiences had one common denominator: I wasn't good enough. My feelings were disciplined, not my behavior. The words and actions of others communicated to me that I was a bad person. Consequently, my shame-based self-perception has greatly affected my family life.

For example, one time my wife, Karen, asked me to fix the gate on the side of the house. Her innocent request pushed my "shame button." Immediately I launched into an unpleasant explanation that I had had a long week, that it wasn't my fault that the gate broke, and that it wasn't my responsibility to fix it! Karen only asked me to fix the gate, but I heard her request as if it were an attack. I felt that if I were really a good person, the gate would not have broken.

Why was I so sensitive to her reasonable request? Here's where my family history comes into play. The truth is, I don't feel good about fixing anything. My past is plagued with strong messages of shame related to my ability to fix things. There are many reasons for these things. One is that my grandfather was a master furniture builder. You could show him a picture of anything you liked in a catalog, and he could build it perfectly. My dad, on the other hand, wasn't good at fixing things, and my family members weren't afraid to tell him so. When it comes to building or fixing things, I'm like my dad.

When Karen asked me to fix the gate, all I could think about was how bad I was at fixing things. I assumed that I'd have to sink new posts and rebuild the gate, and deep inside I knew that no matter how hard I tried, I wouldn't do a good job. Several weeks later, I finally looked at the gate. The latch was loose—that's all! I got two screws from the garage, tightened the latch, and the job was done.

I share this example to show how pervasive feelings of shame can be. Shame causes us to hear messages of worthlessness in even simple requests or suggestions. Then we overreact on the basis of what the shamed little boy or girl inside hears, rather than on the basis of what is really being said. Furthermore, when we have to face something that may prove to be difficult, we have a greatly exaggerated fear of failure. We automatically assume that if we fail to perform a specific task perfectly, we are bad.

One serious consequence of being shame-bound adults is that those feelings of not being good enough spill over into our relationships with our spouse and children. A parent may give a child a withering glance that leaves the child feeling unworthy and unloved. When parents won't admit their mistakes to their children, the children feel there is something dreadfully wrong if they aren't "perfect" too. A husband who rages at his wife, making a "federal case" out of every minor conflict, gives his wife a strong message that she isn't worthy of his love. A wife who mocks her husband's flaws communicates that he is an inept person. Such expressions of shame tear down the family structure and each individual involved.

Shame keeps us from loving one another and accepting love from others. It keeps us from forgiving and feeling forgiveness. It keeps us from feeling joy in life and robs others of the joy they could feel. Feelings of shame stay with us throughout life unless we deal with the shame properly.

Each of us is responsible for understanding the roots of shame in our lives, experiencing our hurts, and choosing to break the cycle of shame for our families and future generations.

Chapter 8

The Myths
Of Religious Shame

Within the past decade, a slow but significant change has begun to take place within the Christian community. It is a change from an image of spiritual perfection to a greater honesty about the hurts and problems that all people, including Christians, face in daily life. For many years it was not permissible for Christians to admit deep hurts or confess personal struggles. Those who dared to share such secrets quickly became victims of what I call religious shame.

Religious shame is a particularly potent force in the lives of Christians. It operates not only on the emotional level, but on the spiritual level as well. It is a shame that makes us feel bad and unacceptable at the core of our being, a shame that communicates that we are bad people, and worse, bad Christians! It communicates an unchangeable personal and spiritual defectiveness. The most devastating aspect of religious shame is that we learn not only to think of ourselves as bad in the sight of others, but to think of ourselves as unacceptable to God. Thus it becomes impossible for us to fully experience the reality of God's love and forgiveness.

When religious shame is active, the church and the

Christian community are not safe places in which to share our pain, problems, and sorrows because we will be judged and condemned rather than supported and loved. As a result of religious shaming, we learn to hide our problems rather than to share them. Yet hiding behind a mask of religious perfection only results in further confusion and hurt. It only enforces our denial and causes our pain to go deeper, leading to greater pain and dysfunction in our families and churches.

The Origins of Religious Shame

Please realize that religious shaming is not something the Christian community has done with malicious intent. Rather, it reflects a flawed theology that focuses on our unworthiness before God, views emotions as unimportant and/or evil, and emphasizes outward behavior instead of the attitude of the heart. Shame-based theology obsesses on our sinfulness and our utter unworthiness. It majors on judgment and minors on grace.

A more common term that describes a shame-based theology is *legalism*. Religious shame and legalism both describe a rule-bound spirituality that emphasizes external conformity to a religious standard rather than a fundamental change in the inner person. Under legalism, spiritual change is imposed and judged from the outside. What is happening on the inside, in the person's heart and emotions, is basically ignored. Spiritual success is evaluated on the basis of external behavior. If you conform, you are accepted. If your life is sufficiently out of control so that you can't conform, you are viewed as a "bad" person—spiritually as well as emotionally.

It isn't difficult to see how we develop a legalistic, shaming theology. The truth is that we are sinful. Without Jesus our Messiah, we are absolutely unworthy. Isaiah 64:6 says, "All our righteous acts are like filthy rags; we all shrivel up like a leaf, and like the wind our sins sweep us away." But that isn't the whole story. We are also made in the image of God! At the foundations of who we are, at the core of our being, lies the image of God. Furthermore, the blood of Christ forgives us completely. It makes us worthy to stand before God.

Just as our human heritage is marred by sin and family dysfunction, so also our spiritual heritage is marred by dysfunction and shame. Our view of God all too quickly becomes an extension of the religious shame and family dysfunction we carry inside. When this happens, we stop viewing God as being personally concerned about our hurts, struggles, and relationship with Him (which is how He is portrayed through Scripture). Instead, we come to believe that He is just another being who must be appeased, so we continue to pretend that all is well.

For example, non-religious parents may shame their children on the basis of parental authority. But when Christian parents use God's Word or Christian teachings to back up their shaming, the effect is devastating. Not only are the parents shaming the child, but God Himself appears to be in on it, too! When we view ourselves as bad in God's eyes, it becomes extremely difficult to believe that God truly loves and forgives. We tend to view Him as an insatiable, harsh judge who considers us to be bad no matter what.

It is tragic to have such a superficial relationship with God when He allows us to be rigorously honest with Him. Religious shame carries serious spiritual consequences, causing us to feel shamed not only by other people, but by God as well! Thus religious shame actually prevents us from experiencing the relationship with God that we so desperately need.

Effects of Religious Shame

Although some churches are moving away from a shame-based spirituality, religious shame is still pervasive in our Christian culture. Individuals who have been Christians for five years or more, particularly those who have been exposed to fundamentalist and evangelical teaching and are older than twenty-five, have probably suffered some religious shame. We suffer religious shame both externally and internally.

When we operate within a legalistic, shame-bound framework, we have a strong tendency to shame others. This is what I call *external religious shame*. For example, it is not uncommon for a Christian who is working through the process of healing from a dysfunctional past to feel anger or even hatred. The Christian who dares to share those feelings with another Christian may well hear a spiritual reprimand such as, "Well, your problem is you need to forgive that person!" Although the statement is true, it carries a strong message of shame and condemnation. It communicates that something is spiritually wrong with the person who is working through recovery.

Another way people fall victim to external religious shame is through unspoken rules that define acceptable Christian behavior. Cathy was a young woman who unwittingly fell victim to this kind of religious shame. As a single woman in her early twenties, she had lived by herself in a Muslim country. While there, she had regularly attended a Greek Orthodox church, the only place she could worship as a Christian in a foreign and hostile culture. Although she regularly attended a charismatic church after returning to the United States, she often worshiped in a Greek Orthodox or Roman Catholic church during Holy Week. Because of her previous experiences, those worship services were spiritually and emotionally precious to her. However, when the leaders of her church learned that she had attended those services, they treated her as if she were a "bad" Christian. Things were never the same for her after that incident, and eventually she had to change churches.

External religious shame makes us hide anything that other people may judge as "bad." Once we learn the hidden list of rules that determines whether we will be judged as "all bad" or "all good," we start keeping secrets. We stop talking about the less-than-perfect things we do, the less-than-perfect things we think, the things that hurt us, and the things that are important to us because we could be shamed.

Thus a shame-based environment makes it difficult to share anything about ourselves. Conversations become limited to spiritualized small talk that reveals nothing about who we are or what we are going through. We become experts at hiding; even our prayer requests have to be labeled as "unspoken" to protect ourselves from shame. Smiling and friendly at church, we return home to sit alone and binge on a package of cookies or work frantically all day and half the night in order to medicate our deep, unmet feelings of emptiness and hurt.

The second kind of religious shame we can fall victim to is what I call *internal religious shame*. This kind of shame is often rooted in our shame-based theology and family experiences. Although it originates externally, it is a shame we carry internally, a shame that we cause for ourselves.

When we shame ourselves internally, we may confess our sins, but continue to berate ourselves for those sins. Thus we never feel the forgiveness that God promises. In fact, we can be much harder on ourselves than God demands. God simply asks us to acknowledge what we have done and seek His righteousness. Often, because we have learned that there is no forgiveness in our families or in the Christian community, we carry that lack of forgiveness over into our relationship with God. We feel that when we do something wrong we have to do a dozen things right just to prove that we're okay.

When I first became a Christian, I felt a great load of shame—a profound unworthiness—being lifted from me. But as I grew older, I had difficulty dealing with post-conversion sin and guilt. Although I confessed my sins to God, I still felt bad, as if I needed to do something more. I felt that no matter what I did or accomplished, it wasn't good enough. I could watch other Christians enjoy the goodness of life, but I couldn't feel that joy myself.

Although I did not realize it at the time, that was my first conscious encounter with toxic religious shame. In time I learned that my feelings of incurable shame before God were a legacy I had inherited through my family and the church in which I grew up. It was a shame that had dictated

Myths of Religious Shame

Shame-Based Spirituality:

1. Having problems is sinful

2. Spirituality means perfection

3. Emotions are sinful

4. Compulsive disease is sinful

5. Fun is sinful

6. Sexuality is sinful

7. Success (or lack of it) is sinful

8. Becoming a Christian fixes everything

Healthy Spirituality:

1. Problems are a part of our human condition. Through the power of Christ we are responsible to deal with our problems.

2. Jesus died to save us, so He alone is our judge. We live by His grace, not legalism.

3. God created us with a full range of emotions. They are not sinful, but the way we handle our emotions can be sinful.

4. Sickness and sin are not synonymous. By God's grace we each are responsible to deal with the sin in our lives.

5. God has given us many wonderful ways to delight in His goodness.

6. Sexuality is a gift from God that we are to enjoy as he allows.

7. God does not measure our faith according to our prosperity or poverty.

8. Salvation is a miracle of a moment; sanctification is the process of a lifetime. Christ empowers us to face the difficult issues in life.

every aspect of life—all family, community, and spiritual relationships—for generations. It was not a healthy shame. In time, I learned to distinguish between healthy shame and toxic shame.

Victims of religious shame are affected by it on many different fronts. I have developed a list of "religious shame myths" that reveals some of the many ways in which religious shame can appear. These myths have generally been given at least tacit approval by much of the Christian community. However, they are all destructive to the individual as well as the Christian community.

Myth #1: Having Problems Is Sinful

The Christian community readily acknowledges that we live in a fallen world. Most of us are aware that we come from imperfect families. These two factors alone indicate that we will sin and have problems. Yet somewhere along the way, we lost the truth that spirituality means we have accepted our need for a Savior and substituted it with the idea that true spirituality means we have become perfect. When perfection is the standard, our problems simply "prove" how defective we are.

As fallen creatures, we do struggle with depression. We do sometimes wonder if we married the right person. We do sometimes want to ship our teenagers off to some unknown place until they are mature enough to support themselves. We do sometimes want to escape life's overwhelming responsibilities. Although these struggles can be a result of sin in our lives, they are not necessarily an accurate reflection of our spiritual health.

In a shame-based spirituality, where perfection is the standard, our options for resolving problems are extremely limited. We can overspiritualize our problems and live as though every problem can be solved through prayer and confession. However, if our problems do not appear to be resolved by this process, we often feel such great shame that we try to live in denial of those problems. Both of these approaches are faulty.

One woman I counseled suffered from depression, ulcer disease, and thirty-five pounds of compulsive overeating. As a child, she had been taught that unconfessed sins caused all problems and that every problem could be solved through prayer and confession. But her father was an alcoholic who brutally abused her physically and emotionally. When she couldn't pray those problems away, she felt spiritually defective, not good enough for God to listen to her.

Of course this woman needed to deal with sin in her life, but she also needed to deal with the trauma in her life. No amount of spiritually perfect behavior or confession would make her father love her or take away the pain of his abuse. She needed to learn to differentiate between the sin in her life that needed confession and the painful feelings that needed healing. Making this distinction is often a difficult process for shame-bound Christians because they have become so accustomed to thinking of themselves as "bad" that they cannot feel the pain of their past hurts, which has great impact on their present problems.

In another case, a man who was struggling with depression attended a church where emotional problems were considered to be sinful. In fact, the pastor openly preached on the evils of seeking psychological help; trusting God, he taught, was the only way to deal with sinful problems. This shame-bound approach forces people to look good and pretend that everything is okay, even when they are falling apart inside. The shame message is clear: People with problems are unacceptable in this body of believers, and anyone who seeks psychological help is hopelessly sinful. Feeling too shamed to share his inner emotional struggles with even his closest friends, his pastor, or his wife, this man killed himself.

I'm not saying the pastor caused this man's suicide. However, we must recognize the powerful shaming message we convey when we view emotional problems as sinful. The way we deal with emotional problems leads to sin, not the problems themselves. When we equate emotional problems with spiritual defects, we force people to struggle

[111]

alone, without the Christlike support that a Christian community can offer.

Myth #2: Spirituality Means Perfection

This myth often operates hand in hand with Myth #1. When we view problems as sinful, we tend to become very conscious of how we appear so that we can convince ourselves and others that we don't have any problems and are, therefore, spiritually acceptable. In other words, we have to appear perfect! We usually accomplish this by setting up an elaborate system of rules that prove our spirituality—to ourselves, to others, and, most important, to God—if we follow them perfectly. We communicate that a truly spiritual person will follow the rules and meet the established level of expectation. Under this kind of heavily structured, rule-governed spirituality, individuals are set up for failure and shame in two ways.

First, if a person has problems, it means that he or she is not following the rules and therefore can't measure up spiritually. The solution, then, is to work harder to follow the rules—read the Bible more, memorize more verses, commit more time to Christian service, and so on. Although these activities are important ways to demonstrate our love and to nurture our relationship with God, they are not the standards by which God measures our value. However, when we are caught up in a legalistic system, we become preoccupied with our spiritual performance and often develop industrial-strength denial of problems that might indicate our failure.

Second, if we don't conform to the rules, we are spiritual failures. A high school friend of mine was victimized by this variety of religious shame. The incident took place during the Vietnam War, when our country was in a period of upheaval. My friend had troubled, hostile relationships at home yet managed to attend church regularly and became very involved with the church youth group. In keeping with the times, my friend let his hair grow longer and began wearing clothes to church that didn't qualify as the traditional "Sunday best." In time, the church leaders confronted him about his appearance and on that basis accused him of being a carnal Christian, a drug addict, and a hippie. The tragedy is that none of those accusations were true, but my friend was labeled as a bad Christian. The condemnation of his spiritual condition came through loud and clear: "You aren't good enough!"

Greatly shamed, my friend dropped out of the church and began practicing the things he had been accused of doing. In time he became a hippie and a drug addict and did not achieve sobriety until he was more than thirty years old. The church is not responsible for my friend's drug addiction; that was his choice. However, the church is responsible for the religious shame that was dumped on him.

Jesus died to save us from legalistic systems of spiritual perfectionism. He is the judge of our spirituality, and He judges the heart, not the outward appearance. We commit great sin in His name when we shame one another by false standards of religious perfection.

Myth #3: Emotions Are Sinful

Many Christians have been taught that it's okay to feel joy or peace, but that other emotions are in some way bad and unspiritual. Grief, for example, is an emotion that is frequently shamed by Christians. Yet it is normal to grieve when we face a loss, whether that loss is the death of a loved one, the loss of a job, or the loss caused by family dysfunction. Often grief is part of the recovery process, and when others shame us for feeling grief—by making comments like "You're a new creature in Christ; it's time to put all these other things behind you"—we have to work through not only the grief, but also the fear that we've done something wrong spiritually.

It is wise to remember that Scripture records a gamut of emotions among its characters. Moses, for example, was so angry that he smashed the stone tablets on which the Ten Commandments were written (see Ex. 32:19). David was so excited when the Ark was brought to Jerusalem that he danced in the streets (see 2 Sam. 6:16). He was also so de-pressed that his bones ached (see Ps. 6:2), and he felt as if the earth had swallowed him up (see Ps. 71:20). Hannah prayed to the Lord so intently that Eli the priest thought she was drunk (see 1 Sam. 1:10–16).

Jesus also expressed great emotion. He gently beckoned the little children to come to Him (see Matt. 19:13–14). He was outraged by the deceitful moneychangers in God's temple (see Matt. 21:12–13; John 2:13–16). He had deep compassion for the woman at the well (see John 4:7–26). He sweat drops of blood when He prayed in Gethsemane (see Luke 22:44). So why do we persist in behaving as though emotions are bad?

Myth #4: Compulsive Disease Is Sinful

This myth has probably killed more people in the Chris-tian community than any other. For many years the church has taken the stand that compulsive disease is solely a result of flawed spirituality—nothing more than blatant, unrepentant sin. Such a viewpoint shames the Christian who struggles with addiction, often impeding his or her ability to seek help and prolonging the agony of the addiction—for the addict as well as for his or her family members.

Like many myths of religious shame, this myth is par-tially true, but doesn't tell the whole story. It is true that alcoholic behavior provides fertile ground for an abundant variety of sins. It is true that it is sinful to try to fill the deep emptiness we feel inside with anything other than God. However, it is also true that compulsive diseases such as alcoholism, eating disorders, and sexual addiction are com-plex behaviors influenced by physiological, emotional, and spiritual factors.

This last truth makes all the difference. To treat only the physiological, emotional, or spiritual aspects of compulsive disease merely programs the addict for failure. For exam-ple, an alcoholic or compulsive overeater often hears advice along these lines: "Give your life over to the Lord and pray ceaselessly about your problem. He'll take your problem and give you the will power to defeat this sin in your life." This kind of advice sounds great. It even works for a few hours or a day. Then the physiological withdrawal begins, and no amount of will power—spiritual or otherwise—takes away those physical cravings. The person becomes totally obsessed with the substance that will satisfy the feelings of withdrawal. The first taste of that substance—whether it be alcohol, sugar, bread, chocolate, or chips—brings immediate relief. Often that relief will lead to a period of bingeing in which the person loses control of the substance intake for days, weeks, or even years.

Whether the compulsive individual is a Christian or not, such a failure is devastating. However, when we limit our view of compulsive disease to the spiritual realm, we set the addict up for a devastating dose of religious shame as well. Not only has the person suffered a physiological and emotional failure, but he or she has once again failed spiritually.

The Christian community has also operated under the mistaken assumption that acknowledging an addiction as a compulsive disease removes one's responsibility for the disease. This simply is not true. Calling alcoholism a disease, for example, does not mean it is an illness like the flu that one catches unavoidably. Rather, alcoholism is a disease with specific physiological symptoms that, if left untreated, will lead to a diminished quality of life and even death.

Anyone who is knowledgeable about twelve-step recovery programs for compulsive diseases realizes that instead of providing a release from responsibility, the program requires rigorous honesty and responsibility. By dealing with issues of responsibility, sin, guilt, and shame each day, the individual with a compulsive disease has a chance to accomplish another twenty-four hours of sobriety.

Myth #5: Fun Is Sinful

Somewhere in the dark closets of our religious heritage, many of us have a list of behaviors and activities that we define as sinful. We then measure our spiritual acceptability according to what the list says we can or cannot do. If we participate in an activity that is on the "cannot do" side of the list, we feel worthy of spiritual condemnation.

For example, when I was a child, seeing a movie—even one like *Bambi*—was considered to be sinful, as was playing cards (unless one used "Rook" cards). And dancing was almost an abomination! As a result, I grew up thinking that I had to weigh the spiritual merits of my every activity. If I happened to have any fun, I became fearful that I had crossed God by enjoying something that I wasn't supposed to do!

My shame-based church experience was more focused on the evil of what not to do than on the delight of God's goodness. Since then, I have had to learn how to feel unrestrained joy in having fun. Today I will not play cards with a compulsive gambler because I don't want to set him or her up for a relapse. However, I have no more of a problem enjoying a game of cards with my children than I do enjoying a game of catch or a walk in the woods. God has given us many ways to have fun and enjoy life in His creation. We add nothing to our spiritual growth when we prohibit ourselves from enjoying the good things He has given us.

Myth #6: Sexuality Is Sinful

We have made a mess out of sexuality—within our culture, our families, and the church. Most of us even have difficulty understanding what sexuality is. Sexuality is more than a genital experience; it is the attitudes and feelings we have about ourselves as sexual people.

A study of God's Word reveals that God values our sexuality. In fact, the entire Song of Solomon focuses on romance and sexuality. If someone were to make a movie based on that book, it would really get attention! Ironically, our sexuality has been the focus of devastating religious shame.

One area of shame has been the mistaken belief that sexuality is nothing more than lust and evil desire. Thus anything even vaguely sexual—holding hands, wearing certain clothes, looking at a member of the opposite sex, hugging—has been thought of as sinful and deserving of punishment. At the first college I attended, a Christian Bible college, this type of religious shame was carried to an extreme. Even holding hands prior to engagement was a punishable sin! Furthermore, such "lustful" behavior indicated that the guilty person was spiritually unclean and irreversibly impure, unworthy of a future marriage relationship.

Unfortunately, the shame of this kind of teaching lingers on. Those who are shamed for sexual behavior often feel unworthy of God's grace and forgiveness. So they go through life feeling as though God views them as second-class citizens who must continually prove their worth to Him. Furthermore, the myth that sexuality is sinful leads to confusion and sexual dysfunction in marriage. When we have been taught that sexual feelings are bad, the feelings of shame don't vanish just because we have a piece of paper giving us permission to be sexual!

In years past, the heavy load of religious shame related to sexuality grew immensely if a young woman became pregnant. The shame of pregnancy was so great for the family and such an embarrassment to the church that the young woman was often sent to a relative in another part of the country until after the baby was born. In other cases, the young woman (not the young man) might have been forced to confess her sin before the whole church. Unfortunately, such confessions usually brought massive doses of public shame to the young woman; rarely did they produce an outpouring of love and support.

The church bears a great deal of responsibility for the tragic loss such shaming produces. We have no idea how many abortions have been performed in order to avoid the unbearable burden of sexual and spiritual shame the church has dished out. The power of sexual shame is very great. Women I counsel are usually afraid to tell me that they have had an abortion. They can talk to me in detail about how they were sexually abused, which is a very difficult subject to discuss with a man, but may go through a year or more of counseling before they timidly say that they have had an abortion. Their fear of further religious shaming is undeniable.

The church is now beginning to take a less shaming approach to sexuality and sexual sin and is finally becoming a source of help and support for unmarried pregnant women. It is tragic that it required a huge wave of infanticide to cause the church to take a bold stand, move out of shame, and begin to offer Christ's love and care to unmarried pregnant women.

Myth #7: Success (or Lack of It) Is Sinful

We live in such a success-oriented society that we even view our spiritual value in materialistic terms. Some pastors and teachers make a direct connection between spiritual health and prosperity. Others make an equally direct connection between healthy spirituality and poverty. God, however, doesn't make such a connection. Indeed, Scripture shows that He uses very wealthy people as well as those who are not financially successful. His main concerns are obedience and the attitude of the heart, not our net worth.

I doubt that Paul had many possessions when he died. There is no evidence that he had accumulated wealth. David, on the other hand, had accumulated considerable wealth by the time he died. Yet Paul's writings have taught God's truth to His people for centuries, and David's psalms have comforted and inspired God's people for more than a millennium!

We can claim no inherent spiritual goodness on the basis of our earthly success. Job's story ought to make it clear that God makes no absolute, directly proportional connection between spiritual value and net worth. Job started out with spiritual value and great material wealth. He lost all the wealth and later gained back even more, but his spiritual value never changed. Material success doesn't appear magically if we jump through the right spiritual hoops. It is the result of appropriate skills, hard work, and good marketing. Likewise, material failure is rarely the result of spiritual failure.

Myth #8: Becoming a Christian Fixes Everything

When we become Christians, we receive forgiveness for sins, assurance of eternal life, and empowerment by the Holy Spirit. That's an incredible gift, but it doesn't turn us into perfect, pristine creatures who are unscathed by the ravages of sin. Rather, God's gift enables us, fallen creatures that we are, to learn how to get better. Chuck Swindoll says it very well: "Conversion is a miracle of a moment; sanctification is a process of a lifetime."

Regrettably, many Christians have been shamed by the mistaken belief that all illnesses, addictions, or problems are supposed to be completely and immediately healed at the moment we accept God's gift of salvation. This simply is not true. Neither is it true to say that healing is directly proportional to the strength of our faith—that those who have strong faith are healed and those who have weak faith are not. This two-pronged myth keeps us in massive denial. It has probably led to more divorces, enabled more compulsive disease, and perpetuated more phoniness than any other. It keeps us from facing the hard truth that our compulsive addictions are out of control, our marriages lack intimacy, and our imperfect families desperately need the healing power of God's love.

Although we can be healed instantly, most of us have to work at it. About 3 to 5 percent of alcoholics, for example, have a spiritual experience that totally removes their desire to drink. Some of those people remain in sobriety for a lifetime, while others relapse into their addictions. Does this mean that God didn't work in the lives of those who weren't immediately healed or who relapsed? Does it mean that they had an unknown weakness in their faith that caused them to fail?

No! It simply means that some of our problems, particularly compulsive illnesses, require a lifetime of recovery. Paul had his thorn in the flesh (see 2 Cor. 12:7). Do we think of him as being less spiritual because of it? Do we believe that if his faith had been stronger he would have been healed? Did God condemn David because he struggled with depression? Of course not!

Our faith challenges us to reach the point of self-honesty—the point at which we can face our sin, accept God's forgiveness and unfailing love, and begin the work of recovery. God does not expect perfection from His children. If He did, He would not have provided grace! Ours is a down-to-earth faith that is meant to be worked out in the trenches of life with the support—not the condemnation—of a healing community.

Chapter 9

Out of Shame, Into Recovery

Most of us, to one degree or another, have fallen victim to toxic shame. It is a powerful influence, often producing tragic results in our lives. It keeps families locked into dysfunction, often for generations. It stands as a roadblock, keeping the addict as well as the codependent from experiencing God's love and caring. It keeps us locked in fear, unwilling—even unable—to take our first faltering steps into recovery. Bound by the lies of toxic shame, we are quick to follow many false roads that promise to soothe our pain and humiliation.

For instance, toxic shame causes the codependent to believe that "if only I do more" or "if only I do better" things will get better. Thus the codependent works harder and harder to "fix" the family addict, which only leads the family deeper into dysfunction. A diligent codependent only produces an increasingly immature family system in which the addict is able to avoid more and more responsibility.

Toxic shame also leads families into denial through an insidious process. In order to survive, the family learns to cope with increasingly severe levels of pain and craziness.

The family members "normalize" the dysfunction and view it as less serious than it really is. A codependent, for example, may shrug off a spouse's drunkenness by saying, "It's only beer, not liquor!" But denial only leads to higher levels of chronic tension and inner pain.

Toxic shame also leads Christians to adhere to legalistic formulas that define the standards for spiritual, and therefore psychological, success. We convince ourselves that if we pray enough, if we read the Bible enough, if we evangelize enough, and if we love enough, life's difficulties will fade away. The only problem is that when the formulas don't work the way we feel they should, we not only have to cope with the painful realities of life but are haunted by the dreadful fear that we have failed spiritually as well.

Breaking the Bonds of Shame

Despite the fact that the seemingly comforting paths of toxic shame only lead us deeper into pain and dysfunction, it's very difficult to break the bonds of shame. To take the first step out of shame and into recovery is to take a giant step! Taking that first step means we are willing to admit and confront the good, the bad, and the ugly parts of our lives. It means we are willing to begin making fundamental changes in how we live.

Please don't misunderstand me. When I say we must break free from the shackles of shame and step onto the path of recovery, I am speaking exclusively of toxic shame. Many Christians have a tendency to equate breaking free from toxic shame with removing proper shame and guilt. This is not the case. In fact, I find that people who recognize and are dealing with toxic shame have a heightened desire to appropriately handle the healthy shame in their lives. They want to confess and receive forgiveness when they have wronged someone. They don't want to stay in denial, not only because of the injury they may cause, but also because denial hinders their recovery.

Individuals who have been in recovery and working on a twelve-step program for a while usually have a heightened desire to respond to the voice of God. Spiritual matters become their guiding purpose in life; they want to deal with the sin in their lives. In fact, the first three of the twelve steps can be paraphrased as, "I can't do it. God can do it. I'll let Him do it." These three steps are a movement out of shame. As individuals work through the twelve steps, they lose their fear of God and discover the strength, acceptance, and love that He promises.

A spirituality based on toxic shame—on legalistic dos and don'ts—robs a person of this type of intimate, healing relationship with God. The church has unconsciously promoted a shame-based spirituality. Fortunately, some churches are moving away from this viewpoint. These churches are easy to spot. They make a clear distinction between healthy shame and toxic shame. They emphasize spiritual growth that comes from the heart rather than conformity to a legalistic standard. They respect, rather than fear, twelve-step work. They offer genuine support for Christians who are recovering from compulsive disease, and they encourage individuals to step out of shame and into recovery.

The first steps we take into recovery are both exciting and terrifying. When we begin to realize the depth at which our dysfunctional past and hidden feelings have dictated every aspect of our lives, we can easily feel overwhelmed. But rest assured, recovery is possible. It is not something we can do overnight. Nor is it a goal we can achieve in a predetermined amount of time. Rather, recovery is a very individualistic lifetime process. Some of us who are minimally codependent will be able to see improvement in our relationships in a relatively short time. Others of us, however, have much more from which to recover, and it may be years before we feel confident that we have made significant progress.

Fortunately, recovery is not something we have to do instantly, perfectly, or completely before we realize any benefit. Every step we take toward recovery is a step we take away from toxic shame, codependency, compulsiveness, and addiction. So let's look at the basic steps of the recovery process.

The Right Start

Remember the story about the three blind men who encountered an elephant? Each one grabbed a different part of the elephant and proceeded to tell the others what kind of creature they had run into.

The first one reached out and grabbed the tail. "We've got a mighty big snake here!" he shouted.

The second man bumped into one of the elephant's legs and exclaimed, "Where did this tree come from?"

The third man, who was showered with a spray from the elephant's trunk, yelled, "Who turned on the fire hydrant?"

All three men had a vivid picture of the elephant from their perspective, but unless they compared notes, not one of them would understand the true nature of an elephant.

Sadly, a similar circumstance has existed in relationship to the dysfunctional family. For years the physician, therapist, and pastor have all grappled with the same elephant. Each has understood a piece of it but has needed the perspective of the other two to know how the puzzle fits together. Alone, each is hopelessly defeated.

Consider how a therapist, a physician, and a pastor—each working alone—might try to help an alcoholic. The therapist may try to help the alcoholic get in touch with his or her "deeper" hurt, in the hope that the alcoholic will stop drinking. Unfortunately, this approach usually produces only an alcoholic who has great insight into why he or she drinks but cannot stop drinking. Meanwhile, the physician can go on forever treating the myriad physical symptoms from which the alcoholic may suffer. The physician may make headway with hypertension, headaches, or stomach problems, only to have another symptom arise in another part of the body. A pastor may pray for the alcoholic's deliverance and assign pages of Bible reading. Yet a day later, partway through withdrawal, the alcoholic will most likely start drinking again and will feel great shame because of it.

The solution to this problem is an approach to recovery that involves the spiritual, emotional, and physical issues. Our pain did not originate with only one event or issue. It is the result of a lifetime of events that have had emotional, physical, and spiritual impact on us. Family dysfunction is a multidimensional problem that develops through generations of family interaction. Therefore we need to approach family dysfunction, codependency, and addiction from as broad a perspective as possible.

The First Step

Considering the multifaceted nature of family dysfunction and compulsive disease, and the three areas of recovery—physical, emotional, and spiritual—how do we know where to begin? I believe the first steps of recovery must address the physical issues. This means learning to handle whatever compulsive disease is at work in our lives.

In the next chapter, we will deal at length with sobriety, which is the process of achieving freedom from compulsive disease. For now let's simply say that a compulsive disease may take many forms, including alcoholism, eating disorders, workaholism, sex addiction, or even compulsive service to others. We develop compulsive diseases in an often unconscious attempt to deaden the pain and fear we feel inside. True recovery cannot occur unless we address the root issues of our problems, and we will never know what those issues are unless we become free from the medicating effects of compulsive diseases.

Tragically, many recovery programs focus on the spiritual and psychological issues and consider the physical issues to be a secondary importance. This approach will not lead a person into long-term recovery. For example, after I gave a talk on eating disorders at a Christian in Recovery Conference, a young man approached me. He was about five feet, ten inches tall and weighed about 275 pounds. He told me I was the first person he had heard explain that obesity could be due to a compulsive eating disorder that was much like alcoholism. He went on to explain that he had spent sixty days in a Christian inpatient program where he had been treated for depression!

This young man had never heard that he needed the

support of an Overeaters Anonymous group to help him learn how to live one day at a time without eating compulsively. Most likely, much of his depression was due to the large amounts of sugar he consumed each day. The feelings from his past that he needed to deal with would never fully surface until he "sobered up" from his eating disorder. Only then would he be able to face the psychological issues and make headway in his recovery.

Although we must deal with the physical issues early on in our recovery, there is no magic order to the recovery process. We begin recovery for reasons that are unique to each of us. One person may experience a crisis that releases deep feelings of sadness or grief. A difficult marriage may cause another person to seek help. A child may go through a crisis that requires the whole family to begin therapy and recovery. Recurring panic attacks may prompt another person to seek help. For others, addiction may precipitate a need for recovery.

It is okay for people to begin recovery at different points and for different needs. However, one of the initial steps in any recovery process is identifying the issues that are exerting control in our lives. Without this basic understanding, our progress in recovery will be limited. Therefore it is most helpful to identify the areas of difficulty early on, including the role a compulsive disease may play. If compulsive disease is at work, we need to gain control of that area so that we may continue in our recovery.

Support for Making Changes

When we move out of shame or denial and into recovery, we are beginning to make fundamental changes. These changes affect the way we do things, the way we think about ourselves, the way we relate to our families, the way we approach our work, and the way we define our success. The list of changes that may take place in recovery could go on and on because even the foods we enjoy eating, the kind of cars we drive, or the color of lipstick we wear can be affected by our shame-bound, dysfunctional past.

It's scary to begin making these changes. It's scary to examine what we learned from our families as we grew up. It's scary to take a closer look at what we assume to be normal. It's scary to face the unknown feelings of our long-forgotten inner child. It's scary to begin changing how we relate to significant people in our lives. Yet recovery requires change. My friend Dave often says, "If you do what you have always done, you will get what you have always got!"

If we want our lives to be different, we have to do some deep healing and make deep changes. It may surprise you, but the primary way healing and change occur is through a support group, especially a twelve-step group. Of course your pastor, therapist, and physician provide valuable guidance and direction in the recovery process. But the "helping" professionals aren't available twenty-four hours a day, seven days a week. Only God can be available with that kind of consistency! I believe God has enabled support groups, which offer loving fellowship, to be emissaries of His love and care on earth.

As I think about how God becomes real through the support of others, I am reminded of a story about a little girl who became frightened as she slept in her bed one night. Her mother heard her tears and came into her room. The mother knelt down, held her daughter in her arms, and listened as the child described the scariness of her room. The mother than prayed for the little girl, asking Jesus to keep her safe, and then went back to bed.

About an hour later, the little girl began crying again. Her mother repeated the same comforting ritual. A short time later, the little girl began crying for a third time. Exasperated, the mother went into her daughter's room again.

"Didn't you trust Jesus with your fears? Don't you believe that He keeps you safe?" the mother demanded.

"Yes," the little girl said, between sobs. "I do believe, Mommy, but Jesus doesn't have any skin!"

During the times when we feel very young and scared inside, we need a Jesus with skin! At those times, God becomes real through the hug of a fellow struggler. He becomes real through understanding eyes and caring ears. He becomes real through legs that are willing to walk beside us when we hurt and shoulders that are available to receive tears.

That's why we need support groups. They provide an environment for healing and recovery. One man who had never before had a sharing relationship with another man said, "I was so afraid to let my sponsor know how I was really doing. I was afraid he wouldn't want to have anything to do with me again. But when I told him that, he said, 'Is that what's been bothering you?' and gave me a big hug! Then he told me about the time in his recovery when he felt exactly the same way!"

Support groups offer a compassionate and understanding ear. One woman who attended an Adult Children of Alcoholics meeting said, "I could not believe a whole room full of people had the same kind of hurt I have had."

Support groups help us muster the courage to make the right, and often difficult, changes. A codependent woman who attended her first support group said, "I never realized that it's okay to set a boundary. I never knew that I don't have to take my husband's rage. I didn't realize that so many others struggle with the same helplessness I feel."

Making a Healing Connection

Once we develop a strong framework of support and foundation of sobriety, we can begin to do the deep inner work of recovery. This inner work involves delving into family-of-origin issues, becoming connected with the feelings of the inner child, and rebuilding damaged boundaries so that we can make appropriate changes in our lives. The inner work of recovery is an all-pervasive process that affects us spiritually, emotionally, and intellectually.

Most of us tend to be long on knowing and short on feeling. This means we place greater value on what we know than on how we feel. This tendency is reinforced in our culture, which rewards achievement and performance and offers little acceptance of feelings. Much of our church experience, too, emphasizes "right" thinking and scriptural truth to the exclusion of the feeling side of faith.

Although it is very important to know scriptural truth, we'd better not ignore the feeling side of our humanity. Scripture overflows with expressions of feeling and descriptions of emotional concepts. If we are to be whole people, we need to address both our thoughts and our feelings. It is a sign of healthy spirituality to know spiritual truth and to be in touch with our deepest feelings.

In addition to the cultural and religious influences that tend to create a division between knowledge and feeling, powerful family influences come into play. In fact, dysfunctional families tend to stifle feelings. If we grow up in a family that ignores, denies, or shames feelings, we will devalue our feelings as adults. Trauma in the family also strengthens the division between intellect and feelings. When our feelings are stifled or traumatized, other aspects of our being, such as our creativity and our ability to express or even feel such emotions as joy or laughter, are affected too.

As you can begin to see, healing the rift between intellect and feelings has a great impact on the person. However, the counseling profession has traditionally focused on analyzing past family problems in order to gain insight for change. Unfortunately, this approach is primarily cognitive. That is, the individual understands feelings intellectually, but rarely experiences a release of feelings on an emotional level. The individual may change his or her behavior, but nothing changes on the feeling level.

The shortcut of learning about feelings and changing behavior without really feeling the feelings and healing the wounds simply doesn't work. It lacks emotional integrity. It recognizes the thinking side of the person, but not the feeling side. This is a particularly potent problem because most adults from dysfunctional families have a great need to become better connected with their feelings. They rarely need more knowledge about their feelings. They have had a lifetime of learning how to behave certain ways despite the way they feel. What adults from dysfunctional families need is to *feel* their feelings!

So one objective of the recovery process I am describing is to heal the split between the intellect and the feelings. Obviously if a compulsive disease is keeping us from feeling our emotions, we can't make this vital connection. That's why sobriety is necessary. Furthermore, becoming connected with our inner feelings can be painful, and a support group helps us deal with the hurt inside.

Once we become better connected to the feelings of our past, we are also better able to experience the feelings of the present. As we face our family history, codependency, and compulsive behavior and let go of shame, we not only become more connected with our inner selves and the people around us, but we also are able to experience more fully our relationship with God!

Many people who come to me for counseling are committed Christians and disciplined students of Scripture. Yet they are struggling with depression, anxiety, marital discord, and numerous other emotional difficulties. They have great knowledge of Christ's sacrifice and the forgiveness He offers but don't feel forgiven inside. It is amazing to be able to help a person, who perhaps has been a Christian for years, finally feel what it means to be a child of God. It is wonderful to see a person who has previously known scriptural truth only intellectually begin to feel that truth deep inside.

Change That Makes a Difference for a Lifetime

When we make a healing connection with our inner child, we attack the issues directly and deal with the shame we feel inside. Shame is like a monster that rules our lives. We can talk about the monster all we want to. We can devise all kinds of plans to conquer the monster. But until we actually pull out the sword and kill the monster, it will terrorize us. Inner-child work goes right to the memories, right to the hurts, right to the people and faces them head on. Once we have dealt with the hidden feelings and issues, we can begin to work on a new way of living. We can develop new thought patterns, adopt healthier beliefs, and discover the reality of spiritual truths.

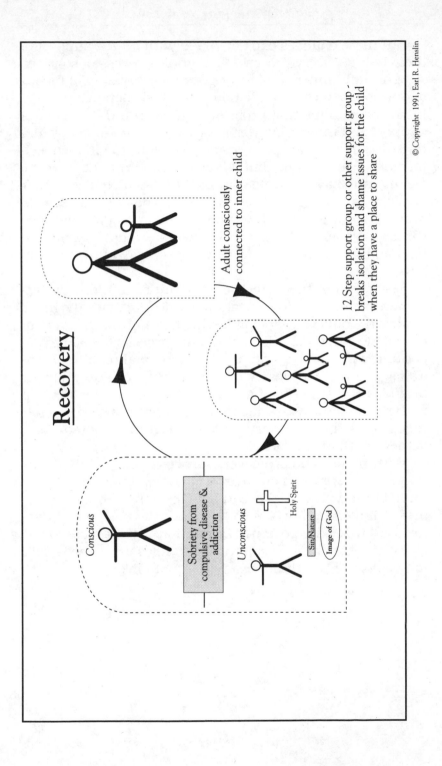

Recovery

Adult consciously connected to inner child

12 Step support group or other support group - breaks isolation and shame issues for the child when they have a place to share

Conscious

Sobriety from compulsive disease & addiction

Unconscious

Holy Spirit

Sin/Nature

Image of God

But these changes can't be made without the support of the whole recovery process. The whole process of sobriety, support, and inner-child work goes together to take us out of our codependency, addiction, and dysfunction.

It isn't easy to maintain sobriety, but within the context of support and inner-child work, it can be done—one day at a time. It isn't easy to discover and deal with the hidden feelings of the inner child, but when we stop medicating those feelings and have a caring community in which to voice our deepest fears, anger, and shame, we can do it! It isn't easy to overcome our fear and allow ourselves to receive and give through a twelve-step group, but when we do, we begin to heal and grow. We begin to be the people God made us to be!

I believe that this threefold program of sobriety, twelve-step work, and making a healing connection with the inner child is the only way for long-lasting healing and recovery of the whole person to take place. This process takes into account the physical, spiritual, and emotional realities. It enables a person to deal with the reality of addiction. It provides the support of a caring community for dealing with the difficult issues and making appropriate changes. It recognizes that recovery isn't something a person can achieve without God's help.

Within the whole recovery process, the healing that makes a difference in our lives will come. It takes work and time, but it will come. We can heal, even from our deepest, most frightening hurts. We can break the patterns of dysfunction that have governed our actions. We can climb out of the pit of shame. We can make changes in how we relate to people. We can discover a new way to live!

PART III

Roadmap For Recovery

Chapter 10

Creating an Environment
For Recovery

I don't believe in the big bang theory of the origin of our universe. I don't think our world was formed when a cloud of miscellaneous gases swirled together. However, I think there may be a valid big bang theory of personal relationships: Whenever people are in relationship, dysfunction occurs!

Most human relationships are somewhat dysfunctional and produce codependency, compulsiveness, and addiction. We don't even have to work hard to develop dysfunctional relationships. They just happen! (At times, however, it may appear that we're working overtime at being dysfunctional!) Merely because we are sinful creatures who live in relationship with other sinful creatures, we will be dysfunctional.

Recovery, on the other hand, doesn't happen by accident. There's no big bang theory of recovery! Recovery is a conscious attempt to heal the hurts we carry deep inside. It is a deliberate examination of our dysfunctional, painful past. It is a concerted effort to change our destructive behaviors and break the cycle of dysfunction. Nothing about recovery is accidental.

As we discovered in the previous chapter, certain steps are necessary in order for recovery and healing to take place. Although recovery is very individualistic, and each person will work through the process in his or her unique way, everyone must work through all of the steps in order to achieve full recovery. One of the essential ingredients for recovery is adequate support. If support is lacking, healing and recovery will remain incomplete.

Recovery Doesn't Occur in Isolation

When we become aware of the dysfunction and pain in our lives and discover that there is a way out, most of us want recovery. We want to heal. But most of us also want to keep our problems and pain to ourselves. Because of the shame we have received in the past, most of us are afraid to share with others what we feel inside.

Recovery, however, takes place in relationship. Our need for support, for meaningful human relationships, is a deep and integral part of who we are as human beings. This fundamental human need for relationship is evident in the earliest recorded portions of Scripture. Shortly after God created Adam, He observed that it wasn't good for Adam to be alone (see Gen. 2:18–23). So God created Eve to meet Adam's relational need.

I find it interesting that even before sin entered the world God recognized and met Adam's need for relationship. At that time, Adam experienced an unmarred, unbroken relationship with God. Adam could be with God. He could talk with God. Yet even in a perfect relationship with God, something in Adam's life was missing. He felt an emptiness, an aloneness that apparently could be met only through relationship with another human being.

The truth is inescapable: Human beings need one another. We are created to contribute to one another and to benefit from relationship with one another. Even Jesus demonstrated a need for human relationships while He was here on earth.

Jesus gathered an intimate group of disciples around

Him. These were the men with whom He was able to share most intimately about the deepest concern of His heart— the reality of God's kingdom. Although He shared the truth of God's kingdom with multitudes of people, the Gospels frequently portray Jesus sharing the same truth in much greater depth with His disciples. Of course Jesus did this in order to prepare His disciples for their future ministry after He returned to heaven. However, I suspect that the human side of Jesus wanted to share these concerns with other men, His friends.

Jesus' desire for companionship and supportive relationships with other men is seen most dramatically during the early evening hours on the night He was arrested. Knowing what the future held, Jesus went to Gethsemane and asked His disciples to sit with Him while He prayed. Matthew 26:37–38 then tells us, "He took Peter and the two sons of Zebedee along with him, and he began to be sorrowful and troubled. Then he said to them, 'My soul is overwhelmed with sorrow to the point of death. Stay here and keep watch with me.'" Although Jesus went to the garden to pray to His heavenly Father, He still wanted His dearest friends to be close beside Him. In the moments before He was arrested, Jesus prayed three times; He hungered for the strength of an intimate relationship with God. Between each of those prayers, He turned to His disciples for support (although they disappointed Him by falling asleep). Immediately afterward, He was arrested (see Matt. 26:39–46).

Those of us who are codependent or addicted and need to recover from the damage of our dysfunctional pasts need to do so through relationships. We are not made to do recovery alone. Yet it's especially tempting for those of us who are Christians to do everything we can to keep our problems to ourselves. Often Christians say, "Jesus is my support group. I share my problems with Him."

Sharing our problems with Jesus is a good first step. He is always there for us. He always accepts us. His Spirit will always minister to us, even in the most difficult times. But it is also important that we feel the reality of Christ's care through relationship with other people who struggle with similar issues. Just as Jesus moved toward His heavenly Father and His friends when He was in Gethsemane, so also we need to move toward God and others. (Let's hope that our friends stay awake!)

A support group is a place where feelings are listened to and respected, rather than ignored or judged. It is a place where the walls of isolation, which have existed since childhood, can come tumbling down. It is a place where it's okay to feel the pain of childhood trauma. Simply by hearing others talk about their pain, we begin to heal. Talking with others often helps us remember our own painful memories and begin the healing process.

The healing environment that a support group provides is truly unique and necessary to the recovery process. It helps break down the barriers of isolation and shame. It helps us realize that we aren't the only ones with scary, painful feelings. When we share our feelings and realize that no one walked out of the room, no one is angry with us, and no one is giving us easy answers, we take a big step out of shame. The child inside each of us has been yearning to be listened to by someone who understands, and the child inside finds healing through compassionate and caring support.

As we progress in our recovery and experience acceptance in our support group, we begin to feel less fragmented inside. We begin to discover who we really are and develop a new sense of identity. Scripture talks about our becoming new creatures in Christ, and as we heal, our newness becomes evident. Perhaps for the first time we begin to feel what we know to be true deep inside. For the first time we may be able to feel what it means to be a precious child of God!

As we work through recovery, we may have symptoms that are more severe than our support group can handle. These may include disturbing dreams that make it hard to sleep, flashbacks to painful memories, a lack of connectedness to our spouse, and other deeply unsettling responses. These symptoms indicate a need for psychotherapy, which is another type of healing relationship. A therapist serves as a guide who helps us work through the deep, family of origin issues. A therapist can help us deal with traumatic memories, develop a new sense of identity, learn how to express feelings, set boundaries, deal with shame, and discover new ways of relating to family members.

Psychotherapy is part of the recovery process but cannot provide complete healing on its own. We may begin to work out the difficult issues with the help of a therapist, but as we face the difficult feelings with the help of our support group, a deeper healing takes place. Together, therapy and support do much to bring about change in our lives. If we are able to add the benefit of an understanding and supportive Christian community, plus an extended family that is not in denial, we're set for deep healing and change!

Recovery Requires Sobriety From Compulsive Behaviors

As I'm sure you have guessed by now, true recovery is not something that happens only on the surface, in our visible behavior. In order to truly heal, we must make deep psychological and spiritual changes. These changes cannot occur unless we accomplish sobriety, which is the foundation of recovery for the person with a compulsive disease. Any attempt at recovery that doesn't require sobriety will be superficial and short-lived.

Those of us who are not chemically dependent can easily be tempted to ignore the importance of sobriety in recovery. But we dare not do so. Addictions take many different forms, so sobriety has many different forms. Obviously, for the alcoholic sobriety means total abstinence from alcohol. For the drug addict (prescription or otherwise) sobriety means total abstinence from the drug of choice. Yet these are not the only areas of abuse and addiction.

Addiction is anything that consumes the focus of our attention: anything that distances us from God, anything that prevents us from facing ourselves, or anything that hinders us from being emotionally available in our relationships. Thus addiction encompasses an almost limitless range of substances or activities—anything from alcohol to potato chips to exercise to gambling. An addiction is any compulsion we become obsessed with, anything that becomes our main attachment and hinders our ability to be in relationship with God or with people.

Admitting and facing my addictions was a difficult thing for me to do. I was not addicted in the traditional sense, but, I discovered that I can become compulsive in a number of areas. I can use many substances or activities to soothe, rather than confront, the pain I carry inside. For example, my primary addiction is food, specifically certain types of carbohydrates, such as cookies, chips, pancakes, or ice cream. When I eat those foods, I end up bingeing. Chips and salsa are to me what alcohol is to an alcoholic.

Furthermore, I discovered that I can become equally compulsive in my work. My farm background taught me that it is normal to work from sunup to sundown, seven days a week. Excessive work seemed normal to me during the years when I attended graduate school full-time and worked full-time to support my family. The sad truth is, those long hours at work usually meant saying no to someone at home, someone for whom I should have been emotionally available.

I am by no means unique in developing compulsive behaviors that are, in reality, addictions. Benign as they may appear, these behaviors are harmful in the same ways that traditional addictions are harmful. Mary, for example, was not addicted to alcohol, food, or sex but was a codependent who had an obsession with Christian work. Her codependency and compulsive behavior, which were related to her family and Christian work, led to addiction. Mary participated in three weekly Bible studies. She was always available whenever her husband, her pastor, her children, or the women in her study groups needed her. She would drop anything to serve the needs of people in her church. She lived at a feverish pace and didn't have any time for herself. Yet she always smiled and was ready to serve.

The only problem was that Mary had to take increasing amounts of aspirin to deaden her constant headache. After a while, the aspirin was no longer effective. Periodically Mary would go to the emergency room and get a shot of Demerol℠ to knock out the pain. Without anyone, including herself, knowing it, Mary became a drug addict. She became addicted to the caffeine in the aspirin and the mood-altering effect of the Demerol℠.

Another person with a nontraditional addiction was Ron. His sex addiction ran his life. Night after night, after his wife and children were in bed, Ron would leave the house, saying that he had to take care of an emergency at work. Then he would drive to a bar, watch the strippers, have sex with a prostitute or another woman, and rush home to bed. The next morning, feeling intense guilt and shame, Ron would pour himself into his work, hoping that he'd be able to stay away from the bars that night. Yet he would go through the same scenario each night. Finally, Ron's wife threatened to leave him unless he entered a sexual addiction recovery program.

Sobriety Opens the Door to Our Feelings

The key to in-depth recovery from these and other addictions is sobriety, not only because it means that we are not practicing our addiction, but also because it allows us to feel our deeper feelings so we can face our hidden issues. Remember, drugs, food, sex, work, and the like are very effective ways to medicate our feelings. If we have a substance to make us feel better, we don't have to face our feelings. If we can do something that makes us feel better about ourselves, we can temporarily ignore the nagging unworthiness we feel inside. In order to truly recover, we must deal with the deep, painful root issues that we have spent a lifetime trying to escape. Sobriety is the first step toward dealing with those issues.

Mary, the Christian service and drug addict described earlier, suffered from deep fear of abandonment that led to feelings of panic. For a long time, the only way she could lessen her deep feeling of panic was to care for others or to take medication. That is why she was so desperate to please everyone around her; caring for someone else kept her inner panic at bay.

After she had been off her medication and frantic Christian service for a time, Mary began to remember her deepest childhood fears. She remembered that when she was a very little girl, her alcoholic parents would put her to bed and start drinking. They would drink at home for a while, and then, after they thought she was asleep, they would leave the house to go to a bar. Mary wasn't asleep. Night after night she stayed awake, absolutely terrified, knowing that she was alone. This was the fear that Mary was trying to relieve through her codependency and drug addiction. Sobriety and involvement in appropriate twelve-step groups laid the groundwork for Mary's recovery.

In a similar way, the sex addict becomes hooked on X-rated videos, pornographic magazines, prostitutes, and/or compulsive affairs. These activities fill an emptiness or bring on a level of excitement that jars the sex addict out of depression. It's not uncommon for the sex addict's behavior to be so out of control that hospitalization is necessary to achieve even one day of sobriety.

Ron, for instance, had to enter a sexual addiction program in order to begin sobriety. After he had been in the program for two weeks, he remembered being sexually abused when he was a little boy. By facing the pain of that abuse, he was able to begin a long-lasting recovery.

The food addict, whether it be the overeater or the bulimic, needs to be free from the medicating effects of food before he or she is able to feel emotions again. Sugar, white flour, or other compulsively consumed foods produce moodiness, depression, and fatigue. These food-induced mood changes cloud the addict's perceptions of feelings and distort the addict's view of what is happening in the world.

In my own case, I have found that sobriety from compulsive behaviors is essential if I want to be in touch with my feelings. When I am not indulging in my compulsive behaviors, my feelings have a chance to be heard. I can almost picture a little boy inside me who is crying out for attention, but the little boy is easily pushed aside when I am overworking or overeating. Sobriety opens the door for that little boy to get in touch with the adult me. It is the golden key that unlocks the door to recovery.

Sobriety and Support Go Hand in Hand

As anyone who has ever tried it knows, sobriety isn't easy. It becomes especially difficult when we start to get in touch with feelings that our compulsive addictions have repressed. This is one reason support is absolutely essential to recovery. To attempt sobriety without support, or to attempt to deal with the feelings of the inner child without adequate support, is to set oneself up for failure. In the same way that sobriety is the key to consistent, genuine change, a support group is the key to continued sobriety.

Unfortunately, many well-meaning Christian inpatient and outpatient treatment programs have ignored the support group's vital role in the recovery process. These programs help a person become sober and may deal with some of the root issues, but once the person leaves the safety of the hospital, he or she is at great risk. A person who has recently achieved sobriety will face increasingly painful issues that are able, because the person is sober, to rise to the surface. Under this increased emotional pressure, there is a great probability that the individual will relapse into addiction.

The right support group, however, can halt the downward spiral when life is out of control. One of the golden keys of recovery is the one-day-at-a-time philosophy that is so well applied in Alcoholics Anonymous. A support group helps an individual face life's issues—whatever they may be—one moment, one hour, one day at a time. The support group or sponsor is available to talk with the addict so that he or she doesn't slip back into the old, destructive behaviors.

Mary, for instance, became involved in two support groups: one for codependency, one for prescription drug addiction. Those groups helped her face the panic that she felt as a child of alcoholic parents. She learned how to deal with those feelings one day at a time so that they would not lead her into codependency or addiction. Her codependency support group was particularly valuable in helping her learn the difference between giving genuine care for others and meeting the needs of others in order to avoid her own feelings of abandonment.

Ron, the sex addict, found a support group that helped him maintain sexual sobriety. For a decade or more, the guilt and shame he felt from his sexually out-of-control behavior had kept him from even walking into a church. But as he worked on his twelve-step recovery program, he made amends for his sinful, sexually destructive behavior. In time, he was able to experience God's love and grace and establish a close spiritual relationship with God that had been impossible before he found sobriety.

Some people need to be involved in more than one support group as they work through recovery. It isn't uncommon for a person with an eating disorder to attend both a support group for his or her eating disorder and an Adult Children of Alcoholics group. I had one client with alcohol and sexual addictions who needed support groups for both problems.

What Kind of Support Group Is Most Beneficial?

Although many different types of helpful support groups exist, I strongly recommend involvement in a traditional, twelve-step support group. Today a multitude of support groups—Adult Children of Alcoholics, Overeaters Anonymous, Alcoholics Anonymous, and many others—meet the specific needs of adults from dysfunctional families who suffer from codependent, addictive, and/or compulsive behaviors. (See Appendix C for a listing and description of established support-group organizations.)

Twelve-step groups are beneficial because they are focused around an active recovery program. These groups have a foundational twelve-step process by which people get better. The meetings are not merely opportunities for people to talk about their problems; they bring people together to support one another as they do the work of recovery.

The purpose of each meeting is for participants to encourage one another to continue progress in their recovery programs. During a meeting, participants offer an understanding and caring ear but also point out attitudes and behaviors that hinder the recovery process. Don, for example, was in recovery and ready to end his twenty-year marriage so that he could develop a relationship with a coworker. His therapist and his pastor had encouraged him to wait at least one year before he made any decisions about his marriage. Don, however, had decided to go through with the divorce, but before announcing his plans, he attended what was to be his last support-group meeting. That evening, a member of the group shared how he had made a dreadful mistake by divorcing his wife to pursue another relationship. A woman shared how she and her husband had worked through recovery together and brought love back into a relationship they once thought had no hope. As Don drove home, he decided to stay in his marriage one more day, which stretched into one more week, one more month, and eventually a year.

During the past few years, some Christian twelve-step groups have been organized. These can be very helpful, but I recommend that a person in recovery be involved in a traditional group as well as a Christian group. I recommend this because people who attend only a Christian twelve-step recovery group tend to have a higher rate of relapse than those who attend traditional as well as Christian groups. I believe there are two reasons for the higher relapse rate in Christian groups.

First, Christian twelve-step groups are relatively new and generally do not have members who have experienced long-term sobriety. Alcoholics Anonymous, on the other hand, has been in existence for fifty-five years, and it is not uncommon for members of an A.A. group to have experienced twenty or more years of sobriety. The record of long-term sobriety is a powerful testimony and encouragement to individuals who are beginning the recovery process.

These long-term members provide an invaluable depth of experience, wisdom, and support to others involved in recovery.

Second, Christian groups tend to spiritualize the recovery process rather than staying at a deep level of honesty and sharing. There is sometimes a strong push for forgiveness before the difficult issues have been fully worked out on a feeling level. Also, the Christian community is just now learning what recovery is all about. Some Christian groups are started by people who want to "help" others but haven't worked through their own codependency issues, so there is a strong tendency to try to "fix" people rather than to share and work through recovery together.

Don't Sell Yourself Short

I know how difficult it is to get up the nerve to go to a support group. It is hard enough to admit to ourselves that we have such deep-seated problems as alcoholism, past abuse, overeating, debilitating codependence, and so on. Admitting such problems to a group of people may seem impossible, but doing so is an essential step in recovery and healing.

When I recommend involvement in a twelve-step group, I don't mean attending an occasional meeting. I mean finding a support group that you can commit to attending on a regular, weekly basis. This is a scary step. Many times a person will attend one support-group meeting, find something wrong with it, and write off all support groups.

Some Christians have complained about the language some people in support groups use, or the fact that people in some support groups smoke. Other Christians decide that a group isn't spiritual enough because the "higher power" to which most twelve-step groups refer is unnamed. As a result, these Christians never become involved in support groups. Often what really happens when this occurs is that the individual finds it easier to see flaws in the support group than to work through the pain and flaws in his or her life.

Even though involvement in a support group may not seem worth the effort, I encourage everyone who wants healing and recovery to become involved in a twelve-step group and stick with the program. Every group has its own personality. Some groups may not suit you, but in another group you may find people you identify with and people whose recovery you admire and respect. So keep looking for what is good, and when you find it, give it your best effort.

The process of finding a support group reminds me of a story about a miner who dug a deep mine shaft on his property. Day after day, he dug and dug. Day after day, he found nothing. But he heard about streams in the hills, where just about all a man had to do was stick his hand into the water and pull out gold nuggets! Frustrated with his fruitless searching and tired of hard work, the miner sold his property. The man who bought his land decided to make the shaft just a little bit deeper. When he did, he hit a rich vein of gold that yielded millions of dollars!

I encourage you to give twelve-step groups a chance to work for you. Don't stop when you're just inches away from the gold!

Chapter 11

The Inner Child:
A Catalyst for Recovery

Young children are wonderful! They are free, imaginative, and spontaneous. They are open to being held, touched, and played with. They delight in playing in the mud or splashing in puddles after the rain. They can pick up a stick and fight off the most fearsome monsters. They can spend an afternoon playing with a whole world of imaginary friends. To them, a dandelion is as beautiful as a rare orchid.

We can't say these things about many adults, can we? As we grow up, the exciting wonderment of childhood grows dim. By the time we reach our twenties, most of us are well on our way to becoming career minded and achievement oriented, giving little thought to the child we used to be. Yet that nearly invisible inner child is no less a part of our lives as adults than when we were children. It has not gone away; it has merely been pushed to the side, shoved underground and out of sight.

Sometimes that childlike part of us breaks through in a burst of creativity or a spontaneous shower of excitement. Sometimes in midlife, the playful, childlike spirit demands attention. It runs amuck, and we buy motorcycles or sports cars, become obsessed with maintaining a youthful physical appearance, or divorce our spouses in order to pursue a new relationship. But most of the time, our inner child remains forgotten, deeply hidden in an unmarked memory.

Although our inner child may be far away from our conscious experience, it is very much a part of our daily life. In fact, the inner child is often in control when we're under stress or facing a crisis. Here's an example. Remember when I overreacted to Karen's request to fix the gate? My reaction wasn't a normal, adult response; it was the response of a scared, defensive little boy who felt shame, failure, and inadequacy. Perhaps you've been in a work situation where the boss suddenly flew into a rage. It's as if someone flipped a switch and the boss changed from a competent, responsible adult into a four year old with a gigantic tantrum! That's the inner child taking control.

When stress hits, we adults turn to the survival and coping patterns we learned in childhood. When that inner child is activated, we can be sure that an old memory or experience with all its feelings of shame has been triggered and is making an impact on our adult behavior. The adult part of us is no longer making our decisions; the shamed, little child inside is calling the shots.

Through the recovery process, we become better able to respond as adults to the stresses of life. Within the supportive environment of sobriety and a twelve-step support group, we begin to become aware of our feelings and to recognize the times when our inner child is making an impact on our life. In order to really make headway in recovery, however, we not only must become aware of the inner child part of ourselves but must also make a healing connection with that inner child. We have to face the old issues that we thought were safely locked away. We have to reach out in love to that hurting little child within and help him or her face the pain of those old issues. We have to forge an alliance with our inner child and together learn new ways to cope with life. This is what inner-child work is all about: making a healing connection with the inner child, which is the catalyst for ongoing recovery.

Family Dysfunction Causes Us to Lose Touch with the Inner Child

A child's spirit is as fragile as it is wonderful. Since every experience is new to a child, a child is always learning. Every new thing, every response, is significant. God designed the family to be a safe haven where this marvelous learning process could be nurtured, but in dysfunctional families, precious little nurturing takes place. As a result, the child's ability to become a whole, healthy person is limited.

A lack of nurturing can occur in many ways. For example, in dysfunctional families, children are expected to *know* how to behave, rather than to *learn* how to behave. Instead of learning how to establish good, protective boundaries, children are often traumatized by parents (or other family members) who violate those boundaries. Instead of learning how to express their feelings, children are often punished for their feelings or are victimized by their parents' inappropriate emotional expressions. In short, children in dysfunctional families are often shamed—simply for being children.

Obviously shaming occurs when a child is abused physically or sexually, but as we've seen in previous chapters, these aren't the only ways in which a child is shamed. A child can be shamed by something as seemingly benign as a parent's overreaction to a given situation. When a parent reacts too strongly, a child may feel afraid but usually doesn't have anyone to talk to about those feelings. So the child, on his or her own, has to make a conclusion about the parent's behavior. Usually the child concludes, *My daddy [or mommy] is right, and I am bad.*

In response to these confusing, shaming lessons, children learn to separate their feelings from what is happening around them—to separate their feelings from their intellect. We call this dissociation. Since they don't know how to handle the feelings associated with these shaming incidents, children make a cognitive decision to cut themselves off from those feelings. They stuff the feelings deep inside, hoping they'll never be felt again.

[150]

To better understand dissociation, let's consider a physical example. When we are severely hurt, such as when we break a bone or are deeply cut, our bodies automatically go into shock. While we're in that state of shock, we don't feel pain. I can remember times while working on the farm when a wrench would slip and I'd cut and bruise my knuckles. Although my knuckles would be bleeding, I could sometimes completely deny the pain. I was in a state of dissociation, detached from what was happening. My mind was separated from the pain so I could cope with the experience.

A child in a dysfunctional family goes through a similar process emotionally. When emotional experiences are too much for the child to handle, he or she will create a division between the experience and the feelings. This separation between feelings and intellect increases in proportion to the dysfunction and trauma the child has to bear. In extreme cases, a part (or parts) of the child's personality will even split off from the rest of the person, creating an adult who has what is known as a multiple personality disorder. But children rarely dissociate to this extreme.

Normally, children simply push the feeling part of their person deeply underground and proceed to handle life on primarily an intellectual level. Sometimes children exhibit behaviors that indicate they have stored away strong feelings. Some withdraw. Others get into trouble, do poorly in school, or develop obedience problems and rebel against authority. Other children develop chronic health problems, such as headaches, ulcers, asthma, or colitis. Still others appear (at least on the surface) to be well adjusted and successful.

Pushed Aside, but Never Forgotten

No matter how thoroughly we dissociate ourselves from the painful feelings of childhood, we can never get rid of them. Those feelings still exist. Although they are far from our conscious awareness, they are still a part of who we are and are very much a part of our adult life.

Consider Tom. He was involved in a competitive racquetball game and was accidentally struck on the back of the legs by his opponent. The hit was hard enough to leave a welt and bruises. The next day, as Tom worked in his office, he felt a deep sadness every time the back of his legs brushed against his chair.

As we began working through this feeling in therapy, Tom remembered a time, during second grade, when he was beaten by his mother; it was anger that should have been directed toward his mother. This particular beating was severe enough to leave black and blue marks on the backs of his legs and buttocks. It also made him very uncomfortable in school. He just couldn't sit still in a wooden chair and concentrate on his schoolwork when he hurt so much. Interestingly, Tom still has trouble with phonetics and spelling—some of what he should have learned in second grade.

Once Tom remembered what had happened, we worked together to help him connect with that memory at a feeling level. He felt the pain, the grief, the shame, and the anger all over again. His adult self reached out to comfort his hurting inner child, and together they were able to resolve the feelings that had been forgotten so long ago.

Afterward Tom was able to see that even though he had no conscious memory of the beating, the feelings from that experience had made an impact on his relationship with his children. For years he had had little patience when his children struggled in school. He became angry and short-tempered when they couldn't understand a new concept. His anger shouldn't have been directed toward his children. Not until he dealt with his anger and began to have compassion for himself did he have compassion for his children when they struggled in school.

We All Need to Connect with Our Inner Child

Tom isn't unique. Every one of us has hidden memories and feelings of shame that influence our daily life. These memories reside in the unconscious part of the person. In fact, the unconscious records everything we have ever experienced. These stored, and seemingly forgotten, memories are surprisingly powerful. For example, how would you complete the phrase, "Winston tastes good . . ."? If you're old enough, you will automatically answer, "like a cigarette should!" Although that commercial hasn't been on television or radio for more than fifteen years, it takes only a few words to prompt the memory of the rest of the phrase.

The diagram on page 154 helps illustrate how the conscious and unconscious selves relate to each other. At the foundation of each person is the image of God. That image, however, has been marred by sin, which injures our relationships with God and other people. Surrounding each of us are the boundaries that protect the person. Since those boundaries are often damaged, they are represented by a broken line.

Inside the protective boundary is the whole person, both the conscious and the unconscious selves. The conscious self is where the adult part of us operates; it is primarily cognitive. The unconscious part is where the feelings and memories of the inner child are stored. The unconscious self remembers everything we have been taught. It remembers every time we have been abused. It remembers every time our feelings have been hurt. It remembers every time we have been shamed.

Although we are not consciously aware of these feelings, experiences, and memories, we still live by them. When we are stressed, when we are in crisis, when we are threatened, when life seems to be out of control, the unconscious feelings of our inner child snap into action. This phenomenon is called post-traumatic stress disorder.

Post-traumatic stress disorder was first identified in combat veterans. A person who has been in combat learns to respond instantly to potential threats, as when he scrambles for cover at the sound of gunfire. After a combat veteran returns home, any loud noise—such as a car backfiring—might prompt the veteran to scramble for cover. The sound sets off a natural survival instinct imbedded in the unconscious that the conscious mind can't overrule.

[153]

Conscious

Alcoholism, drug addiction. eating disorders, sexual addiction, work addiction, religious addiction, co-dependency - compulsive TV, etc. - All numb and anesthetize feeling - also interfere with all experiences of life - our relationship to God, ourself, and others.

Unconscious

- Family Learnings: From family origin
- Feelings: Hurt, anger, happiness, resentment, frustration, joy, grief

- Shame: Trauma - emotional, physical, sexual abuse
- Memories

Sin/Nature

Image of God

The same type of response takes place in us emotionally. An unrelated event can trigger feelings stored away in our unconscious. When that happens, the inner child—not the adult—responds with the survival instincts learned long ago. These feelings can be triggered in the most unexpected ways.

Bill, for example, came to talk with me after becoming extremely angry and defensive when his wife asked him to turn the television down. He was very confused about his anger because he could not consciously understand it. He had been watching television, and his wife had called to him from the next room to turn the volume down. As soon as he heard her yell, he thought she was angry at him, so he started raging at her for yelling at him about the television.

When we began our session together, Bill and I prayed that the Holy Spirit would guide him to the source of his anger. During our session, Bill connected with a memory of his mother, who was drunk, standing over him, beating him with a belt, and screaming at him—all for having the television turned up too loud! The more Bill had tried to protect himself, the harder she had hit him and the louder she had yelled. No wonder he responded so angrily to his wife's request to turn the television down! Her voice had triggered a horrible memory of abuse that he had received from his mother. He had no conscious knowledge of that memory, but it totally controlled his response to his wife.

Situations like this occur in our relationships daily. Probably 80 to 90 percent of our interaction with other people is controlled by our response to old hurts from our childhood. We cannot resolve these relational issues until we get in touch with the deep memories that trigger them. That's why it is so important to become connected with those old feelings and recover from those old wounds. If we don't, they will continue to play tyrant in our lives. Those old rules will determine whether or not we stay married. They will direct us toward success or failure. They will influence how we treat our children. They will lead us toward happiness or depression. They will even govern our relationship with God.

Awakening the Inner Child

Rediscovering and establishing a feeling connection with our inner child is the key that unlocks our recovery. Recovery is limited until we heal the rift between the adult and the child parts of ourselves. But this is not something we should plunge into alone. We need an environment of support and sobriety in order to tackle the deep, painful secrets that our inner child might release.

Once we have achieved sobriety and have become involved in a support group, we're set up for positive changes. We no longer have to depend on the medicating effects of our compulsions and addictions to deaden our feelings. Some of what we can begin to feel is wonderfully exciting; some of it is dreadfully frightening. Yet we no longer have to nurse our feelings in isolation. Instead, we have a support group of people who care about what is happening inside. Our support group provides, perhaps for the first time in our lives, a relationship with people who can genuinely express their care for us. These people won't judge us for the fearful feelings we have deep inside, laugh at the struggles we face, tell us we ought to know better, or become angry when we hurt.

Once we are established in such an environment, many of us will begin to gain access to the childlike part of ourselves. Many of us will discover that feelings and memories buried long ago are set free to rise to the surface. We will begin to feel on a level that we have never experienced as adults.

Some of us, however, need added stimulus to bring out the hidden feelings of the inner child. Betty, for example, could not remember large portions of her childhood. So she began to look at old family photographs and drive by houses where she had lived as a child. As she did this, some of her forgotten memories came to the surface. She remembered being sexually abused when she was a young child. Once she connected with that memory, she was able to begin making changes in her relationships with men. She became able to take control of her relationships so she was no longer victimized by abusive men.

Another woman I counseled had disturbing memories of her grandfather. She remembered only that he was deceitful, played mean tricks on her, and was manipulative. When he died, she felt no sense of loss, just relief. She didn't understand why she felt this way, so she asked family members about him. She then discovered the family secret: Her grandfather had taken money out of the family's estate, which had caused several of his brothers to lose their farms. Later, he set his sons against one another in business, which set the tone for hurtful interaction between their families. Connecting with these memories helped her understand her feelings about her grandfather and her inability to trust men.

Talking with family members doesn't always provide complete answers. Some family members will become upset or angry when questions are raised. If this occurs, a family secret exists. Although we may never know what the secret is, we can be sure that pain, confusion, and dysfunction existed in the family. This knowledge validates the feelings of shame we have inside. If family members don't want to talk, it is sometimes possible to gain helpful information about family history by talking to childhood friends, neighbors, teachers, pastors, or physicians.

A walk through a toy store can also trigger deep feelings. If we listen to our feelings in a toy store, we may find ourselves being drawn to a particular toy. Often that toy will remind us of a specific time period or event in our past. It may also be a symbol of comfort, reassuring even our adult self.

People have always been fascinated by dreams and have often speculated about their content, wondering what hidden meaning they may contain. Many times our dreams lead us to old hurts and distant memories. By writing down the content of our dreams, we can sometimes discover clues about the feelings of our inner child.

Creative activity also helps us get in touch with our feelings. As we practice expressing ourselves through painting, sculpture, dance, poetry, or other creative outlets, the inner child may gain a new outlet for expression, too. If we have difficulty expressing our feelings verbally or in writing, we may find that we are able to express them through creative activity.

Coming in touch with the childlike part of ourselves can be exciting—remarkably freeing and revitalizing. It can also be sad and painful. Along with the good feelings, we may feel the stirrings of hurtful family-of-origin issues. When this happens, we need professional help. Some of the signs that we need help in making a healing connection with our inner child include:

• Crying or feeling a deep sadness when there is no apparent reason to do so.
• Feeling a persistent tightness in the stomach, like a knot that never releases or goes away, or feeling a persistent pain in another part of the body.
• Feeling rage in situations when anger or frustration would be more appropriate.
• Having to be defensive in our relationships.
• Feeling sudden panic or intense fear that doesn't fit the situation.
• Suffering recurrent headaches in certain situations.
• Needing to be in control of relationships and situations.
• Feeling passive and having difficulty taking action.
• Having disturbing dreams or terrifying nightmares.
• Wanting to avoid intimacy or appropriate emotional closeness, such as not wanting to be touched or hugged.
• Having feelings of dissociation, such as numbing, tingling, or dizziness under stress. Dissociation can also include feeling detached from situations, as if we're watching things happen in a dream.
• Suffering overwhelming feelings of inadequacy or unworthiness.

These deep feelings cannot be silenced. If we do not identify them as coming from the inner child and deal with them appropriately, they can lead to more intense feelings of depression, rage, suicide, or violence. It is helpful to be able to talk about these feelings with others in a support group, but in order to heal the wounds that these feelings represent, we need the help of a therapist, too.

Making a Healing Connection

The therapist's role in recovery is to help make a healing connection between the adult self and the inner child. It is not enough to rediscover some of the feelings of our inner child. It is not enough to gain insight into why and how our painful memories came about. It is not enough to excuse or forgive those who have hurt us. The route to healing is through becoming connected or reunited with the little child within who went through the experience—to once again feel that experience as a child and to step into the scene as an adult to help the child deal with what is happening.

Making the healing connection between the adult (conscious self) and the inner child (unconscious self) is delicate work. It combines both experiential and cognitive processes. It is best done by a therapist who is trained and experienced in doing inner child work. Ideally, the therapist should be knowledgeable about twelve-step recovery work. For Christians, I believe it is helpful if the therapist can integrate Scripture and biblical principles into the healing process.

A therapist who is experienced in inner-child work will help a person experience the hidden feelings of the inner child that have dominated his or her life and relationships. The therapist will help the adult and the inner child unite and deal with life together. The conscious, adult self can reach out and help the inner child gain understanding and control. The unconscious, inner child is also a resource for the adult self. Together, the adult and the inner child can handle the weight of past and present hurts. Together they can understand the deep feelings. Together they can heal the old wounds. Together they can set new boundaries and discover new ways to live.

This healing connection is vital to recovery. Alice had been in touch with many painful memories and deep hurts that stemmed from the sexual, physical, and emotional abuse she received as a child. Although she had remembered those feelings, her severe depression and desire to die persisted. A successful executive, she would wander the streets at night, hoping that she would be killed. A committed Christian, she prayed and studied her Bible faithfully. Still, she couldn't get rid of her death wish. Sometimes she would fervently seek God's healing; at other times she couldn't understand why He didn't just take her from this earth and end her suffering. As more of her memories and feelings came to the surface, Alice became more, rather than less, depressed. She had nothing but contempt, anger, and shame for her feelings.

A healing change for Alice didn't happen until her adult self emotionally connected with the feelings of her inner child. Then she realized that those feelings came from the hurt little child inside who needed the love and nurturing of her adult self. Only then did she feel compassion for the wounded inner child. Only then was she able to set boundaries and direct her anger toward those who had harmed her instead of toward herself. Only then was she able to have the kind of relationship she had longed to have with God. Only then did she begin to recover from her depression and suicidal thoughts.

Learning to Feel What We Know About God

Making a healing connection between the adult and the inner child not only affects our relationships with family, friends, and coworkers; it also sets us free to have a more intimate relationship with God! Earlier in this book, we looked at relational toxic shame and how it makes us feel unloved and uncared for by God. Yet God cares deeply about our inner child. He doesn't just care about our intellect. He cares about our heart. He values the precious little child inside each of us. That's why Jesus took the little children into His arms and blessed them!

When we accept Jesus Christ as Lord and Savior in our lives, the Holy Spirit resides in us. Let's take another look at the diagram of the person we referred to earlier. Notice that the Holy Spirit doesn't reside only in our conscious, adult self. The Holy Spirit touches our hearts, too—the deepest level of our feelings. God already knows all about those dark, scary feelings that we've hidden deep in our unconscious. His Spirit within us can help us unlock the dark secrets that keep us in dysfunction, codependency, and addiction. He is waiting for us to take the risk and bring those memories and feelings to Him.

God not only fully knows what is in our hearts; His Spirit is always with us also, helping us make the healing connection we so desperately need. At times, making that connection may seem overwhelming, but God promises His protection. First Corinthians 10:13 says, "And God is faithful; he will not let you be tempted beyond what you can bear. But when you are tempted, he will also provide a way out so that you can stand up under it." The way out of our pain, the way of healing, is to bring those "forbidden" feelings to God and to share them with others who struggle with similar hurts.

A beautiful thing happens to us spiritually when we make a healing connection with our inner child. We begin to feel the reality of God's presence in our lives in a way that we never before dreamed possible. Mary, for example, always seemed driven in her relationship with God. Her life consisted of non-stop Christian service—everything from leading Bible studies to serving on church committees to helping others in her church. She began counseling when it became increasingly difficult for her to motivate herself to go to another meeting or lead another Bible study. She just didn't want to do those things anymore.

Mary had grown up in a Christian home. Her father had been involved in ministry much the same way Mary had. The first time she remembered that he was proud of her was when, at age sixteen, she began leading a Bible study.

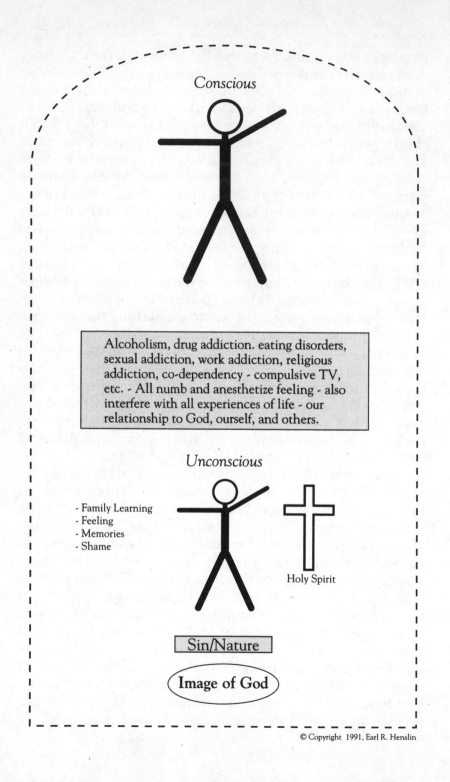

Conscious

Alcoholism, drug addiction. eating disorders, sexual addiction, work addiction, religious addiction, co-dependency - compulsive TV, etc. - All numb and anesthetize feeling - also interfere with all experiences of life - our relationship to God, ourself, and others.

Unconscious

- Family Learning
- Feeling
- Memories
- Shame

Holy Spirit

Sin/Nature

Image of God

She received recognition from him only when she performed as he expected. As Mary began to connect with her feelings of sadness and anger concerning her relationship with her father, she realized that she believed God had the same expectations. She had never felt that God loved her for who she was. She felt that He loved her only for what she did.

That feeling changed profoundly one Sunday as Mary helped out in her daughter's Sunday school class. It was a beautiful day. Big, fluffy, white clouds drifted across a bright blue sky. A gentle breeze carried the faint scent of newly blossomed flowers. The class of five-year-old boys and girls sat under the trees and sang "Jesus Loves Me." Mary sang and remembered how, when she was a little girl, she would watch the clouds and dream of how grand life would be. As she sang the words, "Jesus loves me, this I know," tears began to stream down her face. For the first time in her life, Mary felt that Jesus truly loved her. She had connected not only with her inner child, but also with her heavenly Father!

Getting in touch with the inner child and healing from the hurtful memories that the inner child holds is the catalyst for long-term recovery. Any attempt we make to recover without delving to this deepest level will be incomplete. Once we have allied ourselves with our hurting inner child, however, our course is set for continued growth and healing in all of our relationships. The next few chapters will show you how several people have taken steps out of shame and into recovery. You will see how they began to make changes that broke the cycle of dysfunction for themselves and for their families. You will see the hope and joy that such healing brings.

Chapter 12

A Story of Recovery
From Family Shame

I wish I could list four easy steps that would guarantee a complete and permanent recovery from toxic shame. But recovery isn't that easy. The roots of shame grow deep within us, secretly controlling our every relationship and activity. But we don't have to live in the death-grip of toxic shame. We can take steps to recover from the wounds of shame.

We can loosen the grip of shame so that it interferes with daily life less and less. We can learn to deal with attacks of toxic shame and ward off their debilitating impact. Through a process of healing and recovery from shame, we can become free to be emotionally available in our relationships. To help you understand what is involved in recovery from the subtle yet controlling force of shame, I'd like to share some highlights from one family's recovery.

The parents, Martin and Ronda, were in their early forties. They had been married for fifteen years and had two children—Mary was twelve; Jack was fourteen. Both parents grew up in Christian homes and had always been active in church. At first glance, they looked like a model Christian family. The only apparent problem was that Jack was having trouble in school and was becoming increasingly defensive and reactive at home.

The Warning Signs of Shame

When Martin and Ronda first came to see me, they were very embarrassed. They felt as if they had done something wrong just by seeking help. They didn't even tell their parents that their family was going to counseling, because the little they had shared previously had resulted in defensive reactions from their parents. In their parents' minds, expressing a need for counseling was interpreted as an accusation of failure. It was clear that talking about feelings of hurt wasn't acceptable to their parents. This was an early indication that shame played a strong role in the extended family.

Despite this resistance to seeking help, Martin and Ronda were at a loss to know what to do about Jack, so they sought help anyway. They had read a number of parenting and self-help books by Christian as well as nonChristian authors, so they were becoming aware that some dysfunction existed in their family as well as in their families of origin. Although they were beginning to face some of these family issues, they thought Jack was the only family member with a problem. As I learned more about the family, however, it became apparent that Jack wasn't the only one who suffered emotional pain.

Martin worked hard to succeed in the corporate world. He was out of town on business a minimum of two days a week. When he was home, he always seemed busy—using the home computer to catch up on office work, doing home repairs, or being involved in some church function. Ronda, in turn, had adapted to Martin's absence by developing a tight circle of women friends who provided her primary emotional support. In the children's eyes, their parents seemed to lead separate lives and didn't appear to be as close as they remembered. Mary was a quiet, straight-A student, but Jack seemed to be the opposite.

In fact, Jack's troublesome behavior seemed to be the

main activity that produced interaction between family members. When he stirred things up, a typical interaction would proceed like this:

Martin (angrily): How in the world could you forget to turn in your homework? You should know better than that! How stupid can you be? Mary always gets her work in on time.

Jack (defensively): I'm never good enough for you. You're never home anyway. All you care about is work and church. Mary does everything right! You never yell at her!

Martin: I never have to! Besides, I work hard to provide for you, and you don't appreciate what I do!

Ronda: Martin, you are talking too loud to Jack. There's no need to yell at him. He had a lot on his mind that day. I hate it when you talk to him like that. Why do you do it?

Martin (to Ronda): You never support me in anything! You just cut me down in front of the kids! Do you know how humiliating that is?

Mary says nothing. She just slides further down into her chair.

In most families, a homework problem would be solved without much trouble. But in this family, simple problems quickly escalate into big issues. The interaction just described did nothing to resolve the homework issue. In fact, the discussion about homework led the family deep into a cycle of shame. A great deal of anger and defensiveness was expressed, but the initial issue—late homework—was never resolved.

In shame-bound families, arguments typically go on and on. Often the original issue is lost in the shame fracas. Anger, blame, and defensiveness on a variety of issues seem to spring out of nowhere. Family members stop listening to each other and start defending and blaming. They withdraw their normal affection and find it impossible to compromise without losing face. Sadly, it takes only a few words to start the shame cycle. Once it starts, defensiveness and further shaming prevail—for days, months, or even years.

Shame by Blame and Comparison

Shame cycles can start in many different ways, prompted by any family member. In this situation, Martin starts the shame cycle by angrily confronting his son. At times, confrontation between family members is necessary and is not necessarily bad. However, Martin and Jack do not have a good emotional bond. Since the emotional bridge between father and son doesn't exist, the confrontation leads to defensiveness and blaming rather than to resolution.

The lack of emotional bonding isn't the only problem in Martin's approach to confronting Jack about his late homework. From the beginning, Martin heaps shame on his son. He makes Jack feel as if he is no good, that he can't do anything right.

His first words are, "How in the world . . . ?" Right away, Jack's defenses are triggered. When his father continues with statements like "You should know better" and "How stupid can you be?" Jack naturally feels a compelling need to defend and protect himself. As far as the resolution to the homework problem is concerned, the conversation is already over. Still, Martin doesn't know when to stop. He continues to shame Jack by comparing him to Mary.

Comparing one child to another is a shaming experience that only intensifies a person's defensiveness. Most of us—adults as well as children—fall into the trap of comparison. We want to know how we're doing. When shame is active in our lives, we want to know if we're really as bad as we think we are, or if by some stroke of luck we're actually better than someone else!

Garrison Keillor, of Lake Wobegon fame, understands this facet of human character well. In one of his stories, he tells about the terrible turmoil that resulted in Lake Wobegon when the town drunk got sober. For years the drunk had served as everyone's measure of what "bad" was. Suddenly, when he became sober, the town people had no way to measure their own goodness!

Martin's two shaming tactics of blame and comparison have set the tone for the rest of the family's interaction. The gateway is wide open for further shaming, anger, blame, and defensiveness. Only a person with very strong emotional boundaries could resist the bait and avoid the shame cycle, and Jack is in no position to do so. Generally a teenager can progress no further emotionally than his or her parents. If a parent is stuck in shame, the teenager will be also. However, a teenager's emotional development may progress beyond that of his or her parents if good outside influence from a mentor—such as a pastor, youth leader, or older relative—is available.

Angry, Defensive Responses to Shame

Jack's angry response, "I'm never good enough for you. You're never home anyway. All you care about is work and church," is typical of the interaction found in shame-bound families. Family members are so busy reacting and defending that real needs and feelings become lost in the confusion. When family members attempt to express those real needs and feelings, they have to go through layer upon layer of anger and defensiveness before they can be heard.

For example, Jack doesn't realize it, but his response strikes a deep fear in his father. Like Jack, Martin feels that he isn't good enough. Martin lives under the shadow of this feeling of shame every day. He competes in a dog-eat-dog corporate world, where those who don't produce are pushed to the side. Yet Martin has no idea why his son would feel this way. His confusion only grows when Jack says, "All you care about is work and church." The truth is that much of Martin's motivation for fighting it out in the corporate world is to care for his family. He truly loves Jack and doesn't understand why Jack feels uncared for and unloved.

Jack, on the other hand, feels abandoned by his father. Although he is unable to verbalize it, Jack needs to spend time with his father to find out if he really matters to him. Jack naturally feels shamed because his inner interpretation of his father's absence is that he isn't important or good enough for his dad to spend time with. Jack isn't alone in his feelings. Ronda and Mary feel the same shame of abandonment. On a feeling level, the family perceives Martin as being at work or at church. Deep inside, they believe that if he loved them, they would *feel* like they were important to him.

Jack then closes his defense with the words, "Mary does everything right. You never yell at her!" It's sad, but caring in this family is measured by an absence of yelling. Because Jack is yelled at, he feels unloved and shamed. He even shames himself by continuing the unfavorable comparison with his sister that his father initiated.

Now it's Martin's turn. He began this confrontation with shame and defensiveness and received the same from Jack. He now proceeds to "nuke" Jack with more shame. He affirms Jack's unworthiness by replying that Mary is so good that he never has to yell at her. Martin bolsters his own ego and steps further into shame by pointing out how hard he works to provide for his family. Then he gives Jack a final "slam dunk" with the cold accusation, "You don't appreciate what I do for you!"

What's a Wife to Do?

By this time, the shame cycle is in full swing. Ronda, who has been silent up to this point, can't take any more. She doesn't realize it, but the argument between her husband and son has triggered old memories of arguments between her mother and father. When she was Jack's age, she would step in to stop the ugly fights between her parents. Afterward she would comfort her father. So flushed and fearful, just as she felt when she was a teenager, Ronda tells Martin to stop.

Ronda doesn't intend to hurt or shame Martin, but she clearly jumps into a no-win situation. If she sides with her husband, Jack's heart will only be more wounded. If she tries to stop Martin, who is deeply enmeshed in a shame cycle, he will only hear words of shame—no matter how gently she speaks. As soon as Ronda says, "Martin, you shouldn't," she triggers a lifetime of shaming messages from Martin's parents. From that moment on, Martin sees and hears only his parents' disapproval. In addition, Martin feels intensely shamed—as if his masculinity is taken away—when Ronda corrects him in front of Jack.

The conversation ends with Martin's shamed, painful response to Ronda. The problem is no longer focused between father and son; it is between husband and wife. The original issue has been forgotten and will remain so until Jack creates another problem in an attempt to be heard in the family.

The interaction between Martin and Ronda shows the intensity of feeling that develops in a shame-bound family. Shame magnifies the hurt and distorts one's perspective. Martin doesn't even realize that he has been yelling. Ronda doesn't realize the intensity of her emotions when she tells Martin to stop. Both of them have lost the ability to gauge the impact of their actions.

Furthermore, this interaction shows a distance between Ronda and Martin. They have difficulty agreeing on how the children should be disciplined. Also, the shame messages they have accumulated throughout their lives have greatly diminished their ability to resolve conflicts in their marriage. It's almost as if their ability to solve problems falls apart when emotionally laden issues arise.

What About Mary?

Mary is abnormally silent in this interaction. It's almost as if she is invisible. But you can be sure that she hasn't missed a cue. She noticed very word, every facial expression, and every physical action. She deeply feels the hurt in the family. She is afraid of the anger, but she is careful not to say anything or let anyone know what she feels. Careful not to upset anyone, she internalizes her shame and fear and channels it into more hard work and perfectionism. That's why she does so well in school.

As we've seen, Jack is the opposite. He gets angry and openly struggles with his parents. Although Jack's interaction with his parents is often unpleasant, it is healthier than Mary's withdrawn silence. Jack is searching for independence and autonomy, which is appropriate behavior for his age. Unfortunately, an adolescent's movement toward independence in a shame-bound family is often difficult. It almost requires that a teenager become dysfunctional!

Mary's behavior may be easier for other family members to live with, but it sets her up for a lifetime of perfectionism and codependency. She is willing to do whatever it takes to please others, especially men. Her model of masculinity is a hard-working man who will be emotionally, and often physically, unavailable. She is not developing good boundaries, so she will be prone to care for others no matter how controlling, disrespectful, or shaming they may be.

Finding a Way Out of the Shame Cycle

Most of us could look at the family interaction we've evaluated and suggest what each family member could have said to prevent the shame crisis that developed. Learning to listen to each other and communicate in a nonthreatening manner is good. However, unless the deep issues of shame are tapped into and healed, family members will invariably fall into the shame cycle in future interactions. This family, like many others, needs recovery and healing from codependency and shame.

If a family is to get out of the shame cycle and stay out of it, the parents need to be in recovery. They need to resolve the shame issues from their past and learn new, nonshaming ways of parenting. They need to get in touch with the shame messages they have internalized. Then they need to discover the shame messages they are communicating to their family members.

For Martin and Ronda, this meant counseling and inner-child work, plus involvement in appropriate support groups. Martin attended an Overeaters Anonymous group because he tended to use food for comfort. Ronda attended a Codependents Anonymous group. In addition, they attended weekly Overcomers Outreach meetings together.

Their Overcomers group was particularly helpful because several other couples who were working through deep hurts also attended. It was healing for Martin and Ronda to share their hurts with others who understood and to hear other couples share honestly about their struggles. Never before in their Christian upbringing had they found a safe place where they could share what was on their hearts. It was healing for them to have a place where they were accepted without judgment or criticism. By allowing God to work through the people in their support groups, Martin and Ronda began to build a solid foundation that gave them hope as they progressed through their recovery.

Shame in Martin's Family of Origin

The shame in Martin's family of origin couldn't have been more evident. His statement to Jack that he "should know better" was a message he had heard countless times while growing up. Martin and his sister had labored under intense parental pressure to maintain a perfect family image. Before every church service or gathering, they were coached on how they should behave. If they so much as squirmed in church, they were punished. If Martin brought home anything less than an A, his father yelled at him.

As a result, Martin was a straight-A student. He was heavily involved in church activities. Yet when he didn't make the school baseball team, his father made it clear that he was a failure. His mother never stood up for him. So Martin's shame tanks were filled with "bad boy" or "should" messages. Thus he had set extremely high standards for his performance and unconsciously judged his children by the same impossible rules.

As he progressed in his recovery, Martin began to identify and feel some of the shame messages he had been taught. He began to feel the impact his words and emotional distancing had on his family. He began to realize how generations of shame and hidden pain were making marriages impossible for other children of his generation. He began to see the casualties of family dysfunction and shame (in this case, divorces) strike very close to home. He began to see that he was responsible for making changes in his life, that his wife and children weren't to blame for his pain. Supported by other Christians in recovery, he no longer medicated his feelings with food. The time was right for Martin to start facing the hurt and shame of the little boy inside.

In our counseling sessions, I asked Martin to focus on images of himself as a little boy. When Martin's image of himself as a little boy was clearly in mind, we did various exercises that helped him establish an emotional connection between his adult self and his inner child. We worked through many memories of pain and shame. Throughout the process, we also affirmed the positive messages of Christ's love and acceptance. This is one image of himself, at age eleven, that Martin described:

> I see a boy who looks so sad and disappointed. He didn't make the baseball team. He is so sad and ashamed. He is standing there with his head hanging down. My dad is pointing at him. He is saying that the boy should have tried harder, that if he had tried harder and not been so lazy, he would have made the team. My dad says that if he only worked as hard as the little boy did on baseball, that our family wouldn't have any money. We wouldn't even have food to eat.

It was hard enough for Martin to face the disappointment of not making the baseball team without the added burden of his father's shame messages. Although these shame messages propelled Martin into success in business, they also created endless pain in his life. He became obsessed with work and was unable to establish a balance between work and family life. He also became unable to care for himself emotionally. His best efforts went into his work, while he, his wife, and his children survived on the leftovers. Here's how this particular session continued:

Earl: What would the adult you like to do for that little boy?
Martin: I want to help and protect him.
Earl: Ask the little boy if it's okay for you to touch his

shoulder. If he's too scared for you to touch him, that's okay; it just means he's too badly hurt to trust anybody.

Martin: He wants me to touch his shoulder. (As the adult Martin imagines himself reaching out to the little boy, tears begin to stream down his face.) Uh-oh, the little boy will be in trouble now. His dad gets mad when he cries.

Earl: You can help that little boy now. He needs to set some boundaries between himself and his dad. Can you imagine a glass dome coming down to protect you and the little boy? With that glass dome in place, no one can say anything to hurt you unless you let those words come in.

Martin: The little boy is clutching my hand now. He's afraid of his father.

Earl: We can help that little boy so he doesn't have to be afraid. Stand next to the little boy, safe under the glass dome, and let yourself feel the warmth of Christ's presence. Let that warmth move from the top of your head and the top of the little boy's head right down to your feet. Feel Christ's warmth melt away the sting and shame of your father's words. Feel all of that shame melt into a pool at your feet. (As Martin began to feel the shame drain away from him, his tears were replaced with a warm smile.)

Now the adult you can put that pool of shame into a container and send it far away to where it belongs—right at your father's feet. Take the little boy's hand and assure him that the shame is not his, that it belongs to his father. Explain to him that the shame rests between his father and God and that God knows how to deal with it.

It's time for the little boy to feel some new messages from you and your heavenly Father. Tell that little boy how proud you are that he tried to get on the team. Tell him it's okay to feel disappointed and to cry. Let him see how successful you are today. Assure yourself that it is okay to take time for yourself, your wife, and your children.

Martin: Oh, I've shamed them—just as my dad shamed me.

Earl: It's okay for you to tell them what you just told me. You can ask for their forgiveness. It's truly a gift for a parent to be able to admit his or her own pain and failure and to acknowledge the need for God's help in making changes. By sharing your feelings with your family, you'll help them feel safe so that God can work in their lives, too.

Now it's time to thank the little boy for sharing these deep feelings with you. Let him feel how precious he is as a child of God.

Ronda's Family of Origin

Although Ronda's family experiences were different from Martin's, they still conveyed strong messages of shame. Ronda's Christian family had a big secret. Her mother was a prescription drug addict and an alcoholic. However, the truth was never known outside the family. In fact, church members were sympathetic toward Ronda's mother and faithfully prayed for years that the doctors would find the right medication to ease her chronic headaches.

Ronda saw a different side of her mother's problems. It seemed that her mother always looked forward to the next dose of medicine. As the time for more medication approached, her mother would become increasingly irritable. Ronda would be yelled at if she made the least bit of noise and would then feel that her mother's need for medication was her fault.

As she grew older, Ronda keenly felt the emotional abandonment. She couldn't have friends over because it was too embarrassing if her mother was sleeping on the couch, battling another headache. She was disappointed that her mother couldn't take her shopping or out to lunch like the mothers of her friends did. She felt deep sadness over the relationship that never developed with her mother. She had no one to mentor her as she became a young woman.

Ronda also felt shame and emotional abandonment in her relationship with her father. He was so caught up in the mother's addiction that he was unavailable for the children. He was always taking her to the doctor, getting her prescriptions filled, and rationalizing her angry behavior toward the children. He never took a stand to protect his children against her unjust rage; he merely appeased her.

No wonder Ronda was quick to become angry with Martin! Her husband received the anger left over from her childhood. It also isn't surprising that she was intensely protective of her children's emotional needs and responded so strongly when Martin shamed Jack.

Ronda's recovery process was similar to Martin's. She became involved in support groups and began to feel the shame and pain of her childhood. In one of my sessions with Ronda, we explored a memory that took place when she was eight years old. This happened to be a joint session with Martin, so he was also involved in reaching out to Ronda's inner child.

Ronda had come home from school and found her mother asleep, just as she had feared. She had wanted to invite her best friend over to play, but the last time she had done so, her mother had yelled at both of them for waking her up. It was too risky to have anyone over. Even though she tried to play quietly, her mother woke up about half an hour after Ronda got home. (When an alcoholic or an addict is going through withdrawal, sounds are magnified, so the person is often rather testy!) As Ronda saw herself as a little girl, facing her mother's rage, she became noticeably tense and began to cry. I asked her to tell us what she saw.

Ronda: I see a little girl who is so afraid and hurt. Her mother is yelling at her, telling her that she is a noisy, ungrateful little girl. She says she is a very bad girl, that she should be ashamed for not being more considerate of her mother's headaches. (Martin also began to weep as he heard the shaming and blaming that was happening to the little girl.)

Earl: Can you tell us what happened next?

Ronda: My dad came into the house. I never know what will happen when he comes home. This time he tells me to go to my room. I do, and everything gets real quiet. I know he has given my mother some medicine and probably a glass of wine. He says the wine helps the medicine work better. After a while he tells me to come out and help him make dinner. He never says a word about what happened. (When she explains her father's response, Ronda begins to cry again.)

Earl: Ronda, what would you like to do to help the little girl?

Ronda: I want to help her, but she feels like such a bad little girl. She can't do anything to make her mother feel better. She just makes her mother's headaches worse.

Earl: Imagine your adult self standing next to the little girl. What would you like to do for her?

Ronda: I want to hold her and let her know she is okay. (A new rush of tears begins.)

Earl: Ask the little girl if it is okay for you to hold her.

Ronda: She is afraid of me. She is stepping away.

Earl: Tell the little girl that it's okay for her to be afraid. She has never before had anyone she could trust with her feelings.

(After I said this, Ronda began to relax, and her stream of tears slowed. Martin's tears continued to roll down his face. He wanted to hold the little girl, too. In a few minutes, I asked Ronda what was happening.)

Ronda: The little girl came over to me. She is resting in my arms.

Earl: Would it be okay if Martin held her hand?

Ronda agreed and began to relax again. As Martin held her hand, I reminded her that he cared about her and had felt the shame that she went through.

This session continued in a manner similar to Martin's session. I helped Ronda release her feelings of shame and distinguish between her rightful responsibilities and her parents' responsibilities so that she could begin to set appropriate boundaries between herself and her parents. Toward the end of the session, I asked Martin what he wanted to share with Ronda.

He held her close and said, "I want the little girl and you to know that I feel so sad for what you went through. I had no idea that you were hurt and shamed so deeply. I want to ask your forgiveness for the times I have been angry and yelled at you. I am sorry."

Ronda then began to cry and said, "I'm sorry, too. I know I have hurt you with my anger. I'm sorry."

As I closed the session, I said, "Tightly hold the little girl inside and thank her for sharing such deep feelings. It's special that you and Martin can continue to grow and change in a way that brings healing to you and your family. It is special that you can learn to care for each other with a respect and a gentleness that deepen as time goes on."

New Ways of Parenting

Having gained a supportive foundation for continued healing and growth, and a deeper understanding of the shame they had carried inside since childhood, Martin and Ronda could begin responding to their children in healthier ways. Ronda became less protective and codependent in her relationship with Jack. Martin became less shaming, so it was safer for his wife and children to be close to him emotionally.

As the emotional relationship between father and son deepened, Jack's school problems ended. Martin stopped trying to mold his son and found that he enjoyed sharing in activities that were interesting to Jack. Ronda, in turn, had to spend less energy protecting Jack, so she became more emotionally available to Mary. Not surprisingly, Mary became more alive and developed a new interest in friendships and family relationships. She was still a good student but was no longer obsessed with perfection.

Of course, the work of recovery for this family will continue. Perhaps Jack and Mary will need additional counseling later in life. However, the shame cycle that had continued for generations is now broken. Future generations of this family will be greatly blessed. Jack's and Mary's future children will receive the blessing of parents and grandparents who can freely express their feelings, who know how to laugh and have fun, who know how to feel passionately and deeply, and who know how to support and care for one another through difficult times. They will benefit from a family in which respect reigns and toxic shame plays an increasingly smaller role in life and relationships.

Chapter 13

A Journey
Out of Codependency

Bill Cosby once said, "I don't know the key to success, but the key to failure is trying to please everybody."[1] His words make sense—unless, of course, you're a people-pleasing codependent. If that's the case, his words make no sense at all. From a codependent's viewpoint, success is measured by the ability to please others, and the sure way to failure is to displease someone!

That's how Ann was. She came to me for help, suffering from desperate depression and inescapable anxiety. She was married and had one child. Much of the time her relationship with her husband was good, but when it was bad, it was very bad and stayed that way for some time. Although Ann tried to please her husband and take care of his needs, he manipulated her emotionally and abused her physically. Often, instead of feeling intimacy when she and her husband were sexually close, she felt used.

Even though Ann tried to do everything right, she had difficulties in other areas of life as well. She was a super-responsible employee who frequently worked overtime. Her supervisor would take advantage of her commitment and then criticize her work. So Ann rarely completed a week of work without having had at least one tension headache. She also worked extremely hard to please her parents, who made her feel ashamed whenever she let them down. She was a committed Christian who diligently studied God's Word and didn't hesitate to turn to God for help. She was involved in church activities, always ready to help out. Deep inside, however, Ann knew that things weren't working out the way they were supposed to.

Ann wasn't one to deny her problems. By the time she began counseling, she was already in recovery from an eating disorder and had participated in Overeaters Anonymous for six years. Yet it was difficult for her to take the step into counseling; she was already trying to do all the right things. No matter what she did, however, depression seemed to pursue her relentlessly.

Ann's Family History: A Set-up for Codependency

Outwardly, Ann's family of origin appeared to be just fine. Her parents were committed to raising a Christian family. Her father was active in church; her mother's main focus was taking care of the family. Yet codependency grows out of family-of-origin issues; it's one way children in dysfunctional families learn to survive. A closer look at Ann's family of origin reveals difficulty in handling emotions, abundant shame messages, and parental codependence—all fertile soil for producing codependent children.

While Ann was still a preschooler, her older brother took her into her bedroom closet and fondled her. Her mother caught him in the act and yelled at him, then turned to Ann and scolded her, saying that she was a "bad girl" for allowing him to touch her. The message that she was a bad girl was repeated many times during her early childhood years. Whenever her parents disciplined her, they said that she was bad and that she should be ashamed of herself.

In later childhood years, Ann became more aware of her parents and their relationship to each other. Ann learned to fear her father's anger and was frightened by the control he exerted over her mother. She noticed that her father paid special attention to nicely dressed women at church, always stopping to talk with them. But at home things were different. He mercilessly teased Ann because she was overweight. She saw her parents hug only after they had had a fight. Her mother worried about her own weight and appearance, but was so busy taking care of the rest of the family that she never did anything to improve her appearance.

During those years, Ann developed a special relationship with her grandmother. Ann felt that her grandmother was the only person in the family who really loved her for who she was. But just as Ann approached adolescence, her grandmother died, and Ann felt that loss deeply.

Adolescence brought a mixed bag of memories, feelings, and shame into Ann's life. She accepted Christ and became involved in the church youth group and discipleship activities. She also became one of the best-liked girls in her high school. But that's where the good memories ended. You see, one reason Ann was so well liked at school was because, even as a teenager, her codependency was in full swing. She didn't want anyone to be angry with her, so she tried to please her friends. She always seemed to be doing things for others, but did nothing for herself. Her codependency also led to problems in dating relationships. Afraid of being rejected, Ann found it difficult to set physical boundaries with boys she dated. So those relationships created a great deal of shame for her—shame that she couldn't talk about with anyone.

At home, family relationships continued to deteriorate. Her mother and father no longer expressed any affection for each other. Her mother was angry and depressed; her father, overly involved in Christian service, was rarely home. For the most part, her parents talked to her only when she did something wrong. Her mother didn't even talk to Ann about sexuality. Although her father spent time with her brothers, he didn't have time for Ann. He didn't even hug her anymore.

These highlights of her family history show that Ann's

childhood provided a rock-solid foundation for codependency. At its root, codependency is a response of shame, the need to fill an emptiness deep inside, and survival. Ann had all three of these needs in her life.

As a child, Ann was overwhelmed by feelings of shame and unworthiness. Like others of us who suffer from shame, her inner child desperately wanted to prove her worth. So Ann was driven to overproduce and take care of others in order to prove that she wasn't as bad as she felt inside. Ann also experienced hurt, fear, and emptiness, which she tried to meet by pleasing others. Thus she operated according to the belief: "If I give enough to you, then you will love me." The tragedy is that we—like Ann—rarely feel loved when we operate this way; it is too big a risk to be vulnerable enough to let the good feelings touch our hearts.

Through her early life experiences, Ann learned that the way to survive was to be totally other-oriented. By pleasing others, she avoided many of the conflicts that would have led to further shame and emptiness. However, her focus on pleasing others made it very difficult for her to set boundaries. Her ability to set boundaries was further hindered because her parents didn't teach her how to set good boundaries, and in fact violated her boundaries as she was growing up.

The Battered Boundaries of Codependents

Earlier in this book, I explained that boundaries are like invisible fences that protect us emotionally, physically, and spiritually.[2] If we have healthy boundaries, we have a clear-cut identity. We know who we are and are able to express our feelings and assert our needs in ways that are not harmful to others. Healthy boundaries also enable us to know when we are at risk and give us the ability to take steps to protect ourselves.

Boundaries define areas of responsibility as well. In this way they are like borders between states. For example, I live in California, which shares a border with Arizona. Each state has its own responsibilities and problems. Although

California and Arizona may choose to work together on common problems, the bottom line is that the people in California are responsible for the problems in California, and the people in Arizona are responsible for the problems in Arizona. In a similar way, healthy personal boundaries help us identify areas of personal responsibility. They help us define our responsibilities and enable us to refuse to carry responsibilities that belong to others.

If we grow up in a dysfunctional family, however, we tend to have problems with boundaries. Our boundaries may be damaged, which means we have trouble maintaining them in specific situations or with certain people. Our boundaries may be nonexistent, making it easy for others to take advantage of us. Or our boundaries may be rigid, impenetrable walls that make it impossible for others to get near us. Those of us who are codependent usually have damaged or nonexistent boundaries. Let's look at some of the boundaries that were troublesome for Ann.

Spiritual Boundaries.   By watching her father's codependent relationship with their church, Ann learned that God was someone to be pleased. Her father demonstrated a works-oriented relationship with God rather than a relationship based on grace. The shame-oriented discipline she received from her parents further reinforced the feeling that God wasn't pleased with her.

Emotional Boundaries.   The multiple messages of shame Ann received from her parents caused her to feel totally defenseless against the demands, anger, or criticism of others. She didn't know that she could stand up for herself. So it was easy for others, such as her supervisor at work, to take advantage of her. It was also easy, as a result of her father's emotional abandonment, for Ann to quickly become dependent on a man before she knew him well.

Physical Boundaries.   Ann's physical boundaries suffered a severe blow when her brother fondled her—a blow that her parents never took steps to heal. So she continually had difficulty setting sexual boundaries with men. When she was a young woman, Ann was unable to set sexual limits with her boyfriends and would become physically close to them before a trusting relationship was established. As an adult, she wasn't able to set limits with men at church or Bible study who would give her hugs that made her feel uncomfortable. She also didn't feel that she had the right to set physical boundaries with her husband, so she was powerless to stop his physical abuse and allowed their sexual relationship to be entirely on his terms.

The Inner Child and Boundaries

Ann's damaged boundaries were directly linked to the dysfunction in her family of origin. When her boundaries were threatened, the wounded inner child dictated her responses, making her powerless to set boundaries. For example, if Ann's husband raised his voice during an argument, it would trigger the deep feelings of fear she had experienced as a child when her parents argued. The fear and helplessness of her inner child would take over, leaving her unable to set boundaries with her husband. She would then become a helpless victim of his rage.

At other times, her husband would press for sexual involvement when she didn't want it. When this happened, her inner child's feelings of helplessness and need to please others dictated her response. Rather than saying, "I don't want to do this now," she would go ahead and make love, but feel resentful and used afterward. She had also learned that if she tried to say no to his advances, he would manipulate and shame her until she gave in.

Ann's sexual relationship with her husband was also affected by her experience with her older brother. When her husband began to touch her in a romantic way, that horrible memory was triggered. Ann would feel the shame of the incident and her mother's shaming response. Those feelings of shame overwhelmed Ann and blocked out any positive sexual feelings. As a result, she had never experienced orgasm. Because she felt so bad about her sexuality, Ann blamed herself for the sexual dysfunction in her marriage. This led to even more codependent behavior: trying to please her husband and believing that the success of their relationship was her responsibility.

It's not difficult to see how the boundary-setting problems Ann had as an adult were related to her experiences as a child. Ann consciously remembered those experiences and realized that they were creating problems in her adult life. However, having adult knowledge about inner-child experiences isn't the same as feeling those experiences and doing the work of healing. Ann was doing much of what she needed to do to recover—maintaining sobriety and being involved in a twelve-step support group—but the healing process wasn't complete. She was deadlocked in her recovery, unable to make further progress.

In order to overcome the triggering feelings of her inner child and change her responses, Ann needed to go back to the source of her pain and learn how to deal with it in new ways. She needed to once again feel that pain and establish a healing connection with her inner child. She and her inner child needed to form a caring alliance and deal with those feelings and messages. She and her inner child needed to learn how to respond differently to those frightening memories. Together they needed to learn how to set boundaries in the present. Together they needed to learn new strategies for dealing with fear and anxiety so that those feelings would not continue to propel Ann into codependent responses and behaviors. Once Ann established a healing connection with her inner child, she would be able to move forward in her recovery.

Reaching Out to the Little Girl Within

The earliest hurt Ann remembered was that of being molested by her older brother, which happened several times during a one-year period. The molestation stopped when her mother found Ann and her brother in the closet, but the shame of that experience lived on. So this was the foundational memory with which we worked. It was difficult for Ann to talk about her feelings related to that memory because she felt as if she were a bad person for talking about them. She was afraid she wouldn't do a good job of working through her experiences. As it turned out, however, Ann worked through her feelings just fine!

When we began, Ann saw herself as a little girl about four years old. She was in the closet with her older brother, who had taken her there, and she felt afraid. She could feel him touching her "privates" and could hear herself telling him to stop. He wouldn't stop, and she began to cry. Suddenly her mother came into the bedroom and yelled at Ann's brother. He ran out of the room, but her mother continued to yell at her, telling her that she was a very bad girl. "You should be ashamed of yourself," she said, "for letting him do such a disgusting thing to you!"

That was the end of it. Although her brother had molested her prior to this incident, he never touched her again. Her mother never said another word about what happened, and Ann never talked about it until she entered counseling. Yet the shame messages communicated through this incident laid the foundation for a life of codependency.

While she was growing up, the main message Ann learned through this and other incidents was that her body was not her own. Her brother violated her physical boundary. Her mother violated her boundaries by shaming her. As she grew older, her father violated her boundaries by teasing her about being fat. So Ann was shamed by all of her family members; they each communicated that her body wasn't worthy of respect, that she had no physical boundaries. Even when she reached adulthood, these feelings of shame were easily triggered, making it nearly impossible for Ann to set boundaries.

Helping the Little Girl Inside Set Boundaries

When Ann finished describing the scene in the closet, tears were streaming down her face. She was now ready to make a healing connection with the little girl inside and begin to establish the boundaries that would lead her out of codependency.

I asked Ann if she could picture her adult self standing next to the little girl and helping her. At first, she said she wanted to help the little girl, but didn't know how. So I reminded her how much Jesus loves little children. I read Matthew 18:6 to her, where Jesus said, "But if anyone causes one of these little ones who believe in me to sin, it would be better for him to have a large millstone hung around his neck and to be drowned in the depths of the sea." When Ann realized that Jesus loves children and wants to protect them from harm, she was able to take steps to protect the little girl within who had been hurt by her brother and parents. Here's how our session continued:

Ann: I know how to help her now. I want to take her away from her home.

Earl: Where do you want to take her?

Ann: I want to take her to a castle in the woods, a strong, tall castle with thick walls. She'll be safe there.

Earl: You're right. A castle with thick walls is a safe place for you and the little girl to be. God is like a mighty fortress, too. He surrounds us and protects us with strong walls that will never fail.

Now that you are safe in your castle, would it be okay to help the little girl deal with the shame, fear, and hurt that she feels inside?

Ann: Yes, I think so.

Earl: Inside one of the rooms in your castle is a pool filled with warm water. Take the little girl by the hand and step into the pool together.

The water feels so warm and comfortable. You can use it to wash away all the hurt and shame the little girl feels inside. Start by washing away every trace of your brother's touch off your body. Now you can wash away the shame of what your mother said to you. It wasn't right for her to say that you were bad because of what your brother did to you. You can wash every bit of that shame away. You can also wash away all the shaming, hurtful things your father said about your body. Doesn't it feel good to wash that shame away?

Ann: Yes, but it isn't all gone; there's more.

Earl: Is it from those times when you were a teenager and didn't know how to stop the boys from touching you in ways that you didn't want to be touched?

Ann: Yes. (She starts to cry.)

Earl: Use the warm water in the pool to wash away the fear, shame, and helplessness that you felt at those times, too. Feel the water washing over you, taking all of those hurtful feelings away.

You were not a bad girl for doing those things. You were a girl who didn't know how to help herself. The things that happened to you as a little girl kept you from knowing how to say no. God understands the feelings of fear, helplessness, hurt, and shame you have inside. If you need to ask His forgiveness for some of the things you did as a teenager, ask Him. He will forgive you. Then let yourself accept His forgiveness.

Doesn't it feel better for all the shame from the things that happened to you to be washed away? Allow yourself to feel the warmth of God's understanding and forgiveness washing over your whole body.

As we completed this exercise of washing away her shame, tears continued to stream down Ann's face. But with the tears came a deep sense of relief, a confidence that she could stop believing the shame messages she had suffered under for so long. For the first time, she could reclaim her body as her own. She was beginning to understand that she could set boundaries to protect her body. The next step was to build on that exercise and extend her ability to set boundaries:

Earl: Let your adult self know how you feel about the little girl inside. Tell her that she is a precious child of God, that God loves her, and that He died for her.

Ann: I'm telling her that God is sad about what her parents and brother did. She didn't deserve what her brother did to her. She is so glad that God knows she isn't the bad girl her mother said she was. Now she knows that her body belongs to her and that no one can touch her unless she says it is okay.

Earl: Ann, now move ahead to your teenage years. Picture yourself on one of your dates with a boy who is pressuring you for a sexual relationship.

Ann: The boy is getting very close to the girl. She feels uncomfortable and afraid. She doesn't know what to do.

Earl: Ann, now is the time to stand up for that little girl inside. Allow your adult self to step in and help her set a good boundary.

Ann: Okay. She is telling the boy that she doesn't feel comfortable being that close to him. She is saying that she will leave if he keeps on being that close.

Earl: That's good, Ann. You deserve a relationship with a man who treats you with honor and respect. How does the little girl feel now?

Ann: She feels so safe. It's good to have respect for herself and her body.

Bringing Boundaries into the Present

Ann now had a foundation for setting boundaries and moving out of codependency. She had a place where she could feel safe. She had begun to understand her past boundary issues. She had visualized her adult and inner child working together to set boundaries. It was now time to help her learn to set boundaries in the present, particularly with her husband and her employer.

I reminded her that the Holy Spirit had provided her with a strong, safe castle. I took the image a step further and explained that every castle has a battle room, where weapons and protective gear are stored. I used Ephesians 6:10–18 to help her envision the kind of protection that God has made available to her.

Earl: God is concerned enough about your safety that He

has given you His full armor of protection. He has given you a belt of truth, a breastplate of righteousnesss, a shield of faith, the helmet of salvation, the sword of the Spirit. These weapons and protective gear are kept in the armory of your castle, ready for you and the little girl to use. What do you and the little girl feel you need?

Ann: We both need armor, and maybe a sword to carry.

Earl: Now picture yourself at home with your husband. You are talking together about a problem. What happens next?

Ann: He is getting angry—very angry. Now he's blaming it all on me.

Earl: Remember, Ann, you are protected by your armor. His words can come out of his mouth, but they can't hurt you; they just bounce away. So you don't have to be afraid of your husband. What will you now do to set a boundary with your husband?

Ann: I can say, "I won't talk to you when you are angry like this. We will talk later, when you aren't so angry."

Earl: Good, Ann. Now take the little girl by the hand and walk out of the room. You may retreat to your castle if you would feel safer there.

When you're ready, imagine yourself at work, with your supervisor. What do you see happening?

Ann: He's angry. I did something he didn't like, and now he's demanding that I drop everything else I was supposed to do and start all over again.

Earl: You can relax, Ann. His frightening words will just bounce off your armor. You don't have to please his every whim. You don't have to take his abuse. You can tell him that you deserve to be talked to respectfully and that there are legitimate limits to the work he can expect from you.

After Ann completed these boundary-setting exercises, I encouraged her to practice going through similar scenes so that she could become more skilled at setting appropriate boundaries at home and at work. I reminded her that when she was threatened, she could visualize God's protection through the images of her armor and castle. I also reminded her of the other women in her support group who loved her and would support her as she learned how to set boundaries.

Continuing On in Recovery

Making a healing connection with her inner child broke loose the logjam in Ann's recovery. Learning to establish appropriate boundaries set her free to live in a way she never before dreamed possible. But the road ahead was by no means easy. The faithful support of her twelve-step group played a vital role in helping her make the necessary changes.

As Ann became able to set better boundaries with her husband, he became very angry. When he couldn't get her to respond to his manipulative and shaming tactics, he threatened to move out. That was a difficult threat for Ann to overcome. She not only had to deal with family-history issues that made it difficult to hold the boundary she had set, but she also had to deal with religious-shame issues regarding a wife's absolute submission to her husband. Supported by her Christian twelve-step group, however, Ann had the courage to tell her husband that she wasn't going to give in, even if he left her.

When Ann stood firm, an interesting thing happened: Her husband realized that he didn't have any friends or places to live, so he decided to stay home. She agreed with his decision, on the condition that he become involved in a twelve-step group and begin counseling. He tried to manipulate his way out of those conditions, but she stood firm. So he began his own recovery!

In case you're wondering, Ann's work situation changed dramatically. She eventually got her supervisor's job. And that was just the beginning. Ann began attending school at night, earned her degree, and is now working in a job that she truly enjoys!

Chapter 14

A Story of Recovery
From Religious Shame

When I first met Richard, he was a bright, successful businessman in his early forties. He wasn't without problems, though. He was about twenty-five to thirty pounds overweight, which was increasing his already high blood pressure. Although these problems bothered him, his greatest concern was his battle with depression.

Depression was nothing new to Richard; he had fought it since he was a teenager. Lately, however, it had become inescapable. No matter how well he succeeded at work or how much time he devoted to Christian service at church, he couldn't shake it. Feeling emotionally out of control, he was beginning to fear that he was doing more harm than good to his wife and children. Whenever his children did anything wrong, he was quick to yell at them and often imposed extreme punishment. If his wife tried to talk to him about a routine problem, the discussion usually became a defensive yelling match.

When Richard's parents came to visit, things would get even worse. His father would voice his opinion that Richard should be more involved in church and that the family ought to attend a church that took a stronger stand for the

Gospel. At other times, his father would state that God wanted women to be at home with their children, so it wasn't right for Richard's wife to take college classes (although she took classes only when the children were in school).

Richard seemed incapable of confronting his father when they disagreed, so he never responded to his father's comments. Instead, his opinion of himself would sink even lower, resulting in further emotional withdrawal from his wife and children. His family would then have to walk around on egg shells, knowing that he was likely to explode in rage or defensiveness at the least provocation.

Richard knew he had a problem and needed help, but he had a hard time understanding why he felt so depressed and angry. *After all,* he reasoned, *I am a Christian and come from a Christian family; my parents aren't alcoholics or anything like that. I haven't suffered any great traumas that I can remember. Sure, I overindulge in candy and soda pop, but that couldn't possibly make me feel the way I do.* As long as he could remember, Richard had felt as if something was wrong with him. He had never felt good about anything he had accomplished. Worse, he felt that God was always displeased with him, too.

Like many other Christians who feel a vague, but ever-present, sense of unworthiness, Richard's depression, anger, defensiveness, and overeating were rooted in feelings of toxic shame. He grew up in a Christian home where rules abounded. The legalistic tyranny that ruled the home was reinforced by more shame and legalism at church. As we'll see, Richard's family history reveals the powerful, toxic influence of family and religious shame.

A History of Shame at Home and Church

Richard's father was a deacon in the church; his mother was active in several church ministries. Taking their pastor's instructions seriously, their family attended church every time the doors were open. Every Sunday morning they would sit together in the same pew near the front.

Clearly they were a model family—a family others looked up to. Richard's father, who was adept at quoting Scripture, was respected by the pastor and other church leaders. His mother was always dressed perfectly for every church function.

At home, Richard's well-intentioned parents did their best to raise a Christian family. His father embraced the idea that if you spared the rod, you spoiled the child. So spankings and beatings occurred frequently, followed by talks about how important it was to obey God. An offense as minor as a messy bedroom would unleash his father's rage. At such times he would scream accusations at his son: "You are a bad, sinful child; God is ashamed of you," or "This is the kind of thing Satan makes you do! Who are you going to listen to, God or Satan?" When Richard entered his teens, he sometimes reacted to his father's emotional, physical, and spiritual abuse. Such reactions often resulted in lectures about how the father was God's rightful authority and spiritual leader in the family.

The teachings about the father's role as God's authority in the family and a corresponding emphasis on a wife's absolute submissiveness were strongly supported in the church the family attended. As he was growing up, Richard frequently heard sermons on how husbands were won back to the Lord because of their wives' submissiveness. Yet to Richard it appeared that his father had free license to control and dominate the family, while his "properly submissive" mother was powerless to stand up to his abuse and shame. If she dared to disagree with her husband, he would defensively argue and quote Scripture about a wife's submission to her husband. As a result, Richard lacked respect for his mother and in time became angry at her for her inability to stop his father's abuse.

Yet his anger disturbed Richard. At church and at home, he had been taught that anger was a sinful emotion, that he was to honor and respect his parents, and that most emotional problems were rooted in disobedience to God's laws. So he was shamed and confused by the growing anger he felt inside. However, he had no one with whom to explore those feelings. He had learned that it wasn't worth the risk to ask for help at home or at church. To share feelings was to receive a fresh dose of shame. To ask for help meant to be convicted of guilt. No matter where he turned, there was no understanding—only further shame.

The theology of shame that dominated Richard's home and church life was particularly strong in the area of sexuality, which is of vital interest to normal adolescents. Yet sexuality, as well as teen problems such as drugs and alcohol, was approached from the perspective of God's disapproval and shame. The primary teaching was that sexual feelings were lustful and bad. Young women were taught that if they allowed anyone to touch them sexually, they were soiled and tarnished—unfit for future marital relationships. There was no discussion of normal sexuality, no definition of appropriate sexual expression, and no teaching on how to set sexual boundaries. The message was clear: Anything sexual was evil.

As a result, Richard felt the shame of being a spiritual failure when he had perfectly normal sexual feelings. In fact, he felt like a spiritual failure most of the time and, as time went on, felt more and more unworthy in his relationship with God. The only relief from this oppressive unworthiness came from his participation in sports. He was a talented and gifted athlete who achieved recognition from his family and church because he was a "good Christian witness" on the school teams.

On the whole, it seemed that no matter which way Richard turned or what he accomplished, it was wrong or bad. Toxic shame was a consistent message during his growing-up years. At home, there was no distinction between making mistakes and being bad and sinful. There was no room for learning because he was expected to know automatically what he should do and how he should behave. At church, the feelings he struggled with deep inside were defined as sinful. Anger was sinful. Sexual feelings were sinful. Having fun was sinful.

By the time he left home, Richard had accumulated an abundance of shame messages. No wonder he struggled with depression and sometimes considered suicide. No wonder he lacked respect for his wife and argued bitterly with her. No wonder he was insensitive to his children's needs and feelings. No wonder he felt as though God wanted to punish him. No wonder he became extremely critical and angry with his family, often when it was unwarranted. No wonder things became so bad that his wife and pastor confronted him and insisted that he seek help.

From Knowledge to Recovery

As I became acquainted with Richard's family history, the intense level of toxic religious and family shame he carried became apparent. Toxic shame was a dark force that dictated every interaction Richard had with God, his wife, his parents, and his children. The religious shame was so powerful that it distorted his perception of God. To him, God was a huge, angry man who carried a great big stick. God was mean and controlling, ever anxious to dole out punishment. God's forgiveness and grace were concepts that Richard knew, but could not grasp on a feeling level.

All of this knowledge about Richard's background is helpful, but knowledge isn't recovery. Richard's recovery involved work on several different levels: He needed to identify the shame messages he had learned from his family and church of origin, to get in touch with the child within so that he could begin healing in each of those areas, and to take steps out of shame toward a healthier relationship with his wife and children. He also needed to learn, as an adult, how to set boundaries and deal with his family of origin.

Taking steps out of shame and into recovery wasn't easy for Richard. It was difficult for him to see a therapist. The church in which he grew up taught that psychology was evil and wasn't founded on biblical principles, so it was shameful for him to even think about seeking psychological help. Richard was also afraid of what his father would say when he found out that Richard was in therapy. Although Richard was an adult, he dreaded the thought of facing his father's shame. Because of the way in which his feelings had been shamed at home and at church, Richard also feared attending a support group. It was nearly impossible for him to believe that others would care enough about him to listen as he shared his feelings. He couldn't begin to imagine that he could share his feelings and still be accepted by another person!

Yet Richard knew he would pay a great price if he didn't seek help. He didn't want to lose his relationship with his wife. He was also beginning to feel some of the pain he was causing his children. When he saw them looking at him with fearful eyes, he was reminded of the fear he felt in the presence of his own father—a fear he still felt, even as an adult. As difficult as it was to begin the recovery process, Richard realized that it was his only hope.

Sorting Through the Messages of Shame

The messages of religious shame that Richard grew up with were very strong and deeply engrained. Although he didn't realize it, the messages of toxic shame had become the guidelines by which he lived his adult life. So a key part of Richard's recovery was to identify those toxic messages. Below are some, but not all, of the toxic shame messages that Richard identified. You will recognize some of them as being the common myths of religious shame that we discussed in chapter 8.

Emotions are sinful.   Richard had a hard time responding to his family's pain in a caring, concerned way. Many times he would ignore his children's expressions of need or would just tell them that they were making a big deal out of nothing. If his children cried, he would invariably tell them that there was no reason to cry so much. When his wife expressed hurt or frustration, Richard rarely responded with any degree of empathy or caring. This apparent lack of caring was one side effect of Richard's inability to face or experience his own feelings.

You see, Richard felt shamed whenever he began to feel

emotions, especially those of anger or hurt. As a young boy, he had learned to keep his feelings to himself. If he openly expressed anger or hurt, his father responded with rage and shame rather than love and concern. His father's response led Richard to believe that God didn't approve of his feelings either. He felt that having feelings was sinful and believed that his feelings proved the weakness of his faith by demonstrating his lack of spiritual commitment. No wonder he had trouble handling emotions in his family!

Sexuality is sinful.   Richard also found it difficult to deal with his sexual feelings. The strong message that emotions and feelings are bad, combined with the view that sexuality is nothing more than lust, contributed to a lack of sexual intimacy and pleasure in his marital relationship. Although sex was something he was supposed to be allowed to enjoy in marriage, Richard was burdened with feelings of shame whenever he wanted sex. The message seemed to be that sex within marriage was permissible lust, but lust nonetheless.

As a result, Richard acted as though sex was a duty to be performed, not to be enjoyed. He didn't know the enjoyment of snuggling with his wife and being close to her. He couldn't allow himself to feel the pleasure of being close. Because he wasn't connected to his sexual feelings, he also couldn't understand his wife's sexual needs. He didn't have a clue that closeness and affection were important to her.

Wives are to obey their husbands.   Richard's marital difficulties weren't limited to issues of sexuality. He had an underlying lack of respect for women that was rooted in messages of religious and family shame. He had been taught at church and at home that women were to be completely submissive to men in all things. For years he had watched his mother model submission by accepting his father's emotional and physical abuse. Yet as Richard grew older, she would talk to him about her frustration with his father's control. By sharing her anger with Richard instead of with her husband, she reinforced the message that it was impossible to talk to his father directly. She also communicated that the way to handle anger and pain was to do so indirectly, behind the back of the person with whom you had difficulties.

With these messages firmly implanted, Richard sought to control his wife. He unconsciously regulated her life with incredibly unrealistic expectations and was rarely encouraging or supportive. When she decided to go back to school, for example, he did nothing to ease her load at home so she would have additional time and energy to devote to her studies. As the years passed, the emotional distance and coldness between Richard and his wife increased.

As you can see, most of Richard's personal life was driven by shame. It took a great deal of work for him to begin to identify the shame messages that ruled his life. It took a great deal of courage to get in touch with the shamed feelings of the little boy inside. He could not have done it without the caring environment of his support group.

Drawing on the Strength of a Support Group

As you might imagine, participating in a support group was a difficult step for Richard. He resisted being in a support group for a long time. The toxic religious and family shame messages of his past made it unthinkable for him to publicly share his emotions, especially those of fear and anger. But he finally allowed himself to go to a twelve-step support group for men from dysfunctional families.

Being a part of that support group was an overwhelming experience for him. He had never known that other men struggled with some of the same feelings he felt. He had never seen a man cry until he went to that support group. Although some men in the group expressed anger at God, others rejoiced in His grace. Through his support group, Richard began to realize that God might not be the condemning, impossible-to-please taskmaster that he thought He was.

At times, Richard was quite uncomfortable in his support group. When men expressed their anger, he felt that they should immediately confess it and ask for forgiveness. Yet in time he saw that when men expressed their anger, whether it be toward God or toward people who had hurt them, they were also able to let go of their anger as they progressed in their recovery.

For a long time, seeing other men cry was frightening. When others shed tears, Richard began to feel his own tears welling up from deep inside. As his own tears rose to the surface, he connected with a deep fear and shame: that his father would suddenly burst into the room and be angry with him. But as Richard continued to participate in his support group, he could feel the restless stirrings of a deep part of himself, a part that felt more like a little boy than a man.

Touching the Little Boy Inside

Involvement in his support group had begun to awaken the hurting little boy inside Richard, but reaching out to help that little boy wasn't easy. Deep issues of religious and family shame are not resolved through one exercise or one emotional experience. These issues take a great deal of hard work—reading, study, sharing with others who struggle in similar ways, and appropriate counseling. Eventually, through a number of counseling sessions, Richard allowed himself to experience the feelings that follow.

As we began the session, I asked Richard to picture himself as a little boy. The image that came to his mind was that of a boy about ten years old. As he focused on that little boy, big tears welled up in the corners of his eyes and began to stream down his face. I asked Richard if he could tell me what he saw.

Richard: I see a little boy who looks so sad. His head is hanging down. He is a bad boy.
Earl: Who said he is a bad boy?
Richard: His dad did. His dad doesn't like him because the little boy can't do anything right. His dad always yells at the little boy and never tells him when he has done okay.

The little boy is so bad that his dad won't hug him or love him.

Earl: Do you know why the little boy is so bad?

Richard: He didn't have anybody to play catch with him, so he was throwing a baseball up on the roof and catching it when it came down. It was fun. But one time he didn't throw the ball all the way to the roof, and it broke an upstairs window. Then he was in trouble.

Earl: What happened next?

Richard: My dad ran out of the house and grabbed me. He yelled at me. He told me how bad I was and that I should be ashamed for breaking the window. Then he started hitting me with a stick real hard. I couldn't get away from him. I hurt so much from where he hit me.

As Richard told his story, he became increasingly fearful. He continued to cry, almost as if he expected his father to come into the room at that moment. Suddenly, Richard's emotion changed from fear to anger. He said, "My dad should not have yelled at me like that. He should not have hit me. It was a mistake. I wasn't trying to hit the window. I just didn't have anybody to play with." Then Richard abruptly became quiet and said, "I can't be angry with my father. He says I am supposed to obey and honor him. That's what my church says, too. I'm supposed to forgive my father. It is a sin to be angry with him."

At this point, Richard was trapped by conflicting internal messages. He was naturally angry at his father because of his father's abuse. Yet the messages of religious shame—that he must honor his father, that anger is sin, that he should forgive his father—cut off those internal feelings. Richard needed to resolve those conflicting internal feelings. Here's how we did that.

Earl: Richard, if it would be okay, let the man you are today step between the father and the little boy. What would you then do to help the little boy?

Richard: I won't let him hit the little boy any more.

Earl: What do you want to tell the father?

Richard: Dad, he just made a mistake. He shouldn't be punished like that for making a mistake. It's wrong for you to tell him he's bad just because he made a mistake.

Earl: Richard, would you take the little boy by the hand and take him to a safe place where the two of you can be alone?

Richard: Yes, there's a stream in the woods where I used to like to play when I was little. We'll be safe there.

Earl: Now that you and the little boy are safe together, what would you like to do for that little boy?

Richard: I just want to hold him and be close to him. I want him to know that I love him.

As Richard pictured himself holding and comforting the little boy, deep tears began to flow. He was at last feeling the emotions of a small, hurting child who never had the opportunity to cry. He was feeling the pain of all the shame he had taken in from his father and his church. As he reached out to that hurting little boy inside, he gave him the acceptance, comfort, and grace that he had never received while growing up. Now he was ready to help the little boy set proper boundaries and let go of the shame that had wounded him so deeply.

For Richard and other adults who have been wounded by religious shame, letting go of that shame is a necessary part of recovery. Religious shame wounds us at a deep level and creates a hole in our boundaries—an area where we are vulnerable and helpless to fend off similar attacks and hurts. These shattered boundaries affect not only the child, but the adult as well. As an adult, Richard knew that some of the spiritual teachings from his legalistic background were false. Although he understood this on an intellectual level, the toxic shame messages from his past were stronger than what he had learned as an adult. So, on a feeling level, the shame messages were just as strong as when he was a child.

That's what religious shame does. It becomes an inner block that keeps people from feeling God's grace, love, and goodness. So my goal in the next part of our session was to help Richard find a way to feel the shame leave him so that he could begin to feel what he knew to be true about God.

As Richard pictured himself sitting next to the little boy, I asked him to imagine a protective boundary, such as a glass dome, surrounding the two of them. I reminded him that he and the little boy were safe inside that glass dome. Then I proceeded with our session.

I reminded Richard of how he felt when he first asked Christ to come into his life. I asked him to remember that he could feel safe because Jesus was his Savior. I reminded him that the Holy Spirit had always been with him, even in his deepest feelings of shame. That memory brought a smile of relief to Richard's face.

Then I told Richard how much Jesus loved little children and read Matthew 19:13–14 to him.

> *Then little children were brought to Jesus for him to place his hands on them and pray for them. But the disciples rebuked those who brought them.*
> *Jesus said, "Let the little children come to me, and do not hinder them, for the kingdom of heaven belongs to such as these." When he had placed his hands on them, he went on from there.*

"See, Richard," I said, "Jesus wanted the children to come to Him. He was upset with the adults who tried to keep the children from Him. He said that the kingdom of heaven belonged to children.

"Imagine yourself as one of the children who went to Jesus. Let yourself feel what it was like with Jesus. Feel His arms around you, loving you, keeping you safe. Let the warmth of His love slowly move from the top of your head and the little boy's head down to your feet. Feel the warmth of His love melt the shame away.

"Now the shame is in a pool at your feet. Scoop up that shame and put it into a container. With the help of the little boy, throw that container of shame where it belongs—back to your father and others who gave it to you—at the foot of the cross, where Jesus can take care of it. Now that the shame is gone, you can begin to feel the difference between

God as you knew Him growing up and God as you know Him now." At this point, there were more tears in Richard's eyes, but there was also the beginning of a smile, a smile of peace arising from deep within his soul. He was beginning to feel what it could be like to live without the load of shame that had weighed him down for so many years.

Next I assured Richard that it was okay for him to let go of the shame. (This can be difficult, because the child within often feels sorry for all the people who are part of that shame.) As Richard pictured his father and others standing at the foot of the cross with his container of shame, I reminded him that God knows what to do with the shame and the people to whom it belongs.

"God knows the intentions of your father's heart," I said. "He knows how to take care of your father and the others. You no longer need to carry their shame for them; it is their responsibility. God's hands are so much bigger, stronger, and more capable than yours. Let Him take care of things.

"Your responsibility now is to continue to do the work of healing. You now need to continue to build stronger boundaries so that you can protect yourself and your inner child from future shame. You must also learn to grow in God's grace so that you can express His grace to yourself, your wife, your children, your friends, or whoever may come along your path. You can now begin to take what you know to be true and to feel it in every part of your life!"

As is the case with many adults who suffer from religious shame, this process of getting in touch with his inner child and releasing the shame that he had felt since childhood was a turning point in Richard's recovery. By understanding and feeling the emotions of his inner child, Richard was able to respond to his children's mistakes and needs with patience and understanding rather than anger. Richard became able to listen to his wife's feelings, even her frustrations, and offer loving care and support rather than responding to her out of his own feelings of anger and shame. Richard also felt a new closeness to God. Grace and forgiveness were no longer vague, distant concepts. They became the feelings of his heart!

Chapter 15

Growing
Through Recovery

In the past few chapters, we've seen how the three keys to recovery—sobriety, support, and making a healing connection with the inner child—work together to break the cycles of shame and dysfunction in a person's life. As helpful and necessary as these tools are, however, they offer no permanent cure for the problems of dysfunction, codependency, compulsive behavior, or addiction. The truth is that recovery is a lifelong process. We have to keep on growing through recovery, responding to life's ongoing demands and hurts, one day at a time.

At times, that growth is joyous, at times painful, at times delightful, at times arduous, at times steady, and at times faltering. Solomon's journal, the book of Ecclesiastes, chronicles the ups and downs, ebb and flow of life. His words portray beautiful images of what ongoing recovery is all about.

> *There is a time for everything, and a season*
>   *for every activity under heaven:*
> *a time to be born and a time to die,*
> *a time to plant and a time to uproot,*

a time to kill and a time to heal,
a time to tear down and a time to build,
a time to weep and a time to laugh,
a time to mourn and a time to dance,
a time to scatter stones and a time to gather them,
a time to embrace and a time to refrain,
a time to search and a time to give up,
a time to keep and a time to throw away,
a time to tear and a time to mend,
a time to be silent and a time to speak,
a time to love and a time to hate,
a time for war and a time for peace.

(Eccl. 3:1–8)

A Time to Plant and a Time to Uproot

The years I spent growing up on a farm cause this to be a particularly vivid image for me. I hope it will add to your understanding of recovery, too. Each spring, tractors roll into the corn fields to prepare the ground and plant the seed. The farmers may work for days, but after the seed is planted, there is little evidence of the work that has been done—only the tracks of tractors and the implements that were pulled behind them.

What follows is a process of waiting. There is no immediate gain for the hours of hard work; corn stalks don't pop out of the ground overnight. For days, even weeks, the seed is nurtured underground by the rain and warm sun. As the warmth and moisture make their way into the ground, the seed comes to life. In the underground darkness, it begins to grow. Eventually a tiny green shoot breaks through the ground and opens up to the sun.

Once that tender shoot bursts into the sunlight, watch out! With continued care—working the soil to help the rain soak in, pulling away the weeds that would choke out its life and shadow the warming rays of the sun—that tiny corn shoot explodes into growth. If conditions are right, it will grow inches in a day! Farmers even talk about being able to hear corn grow during the night. After the growth comes a bountiful harvest.

In a similar way, the beginning of recovery requires much hard work—work like plowing the soil, tossing away rocks that clutter the field, and planting the seed. For a while, it may seem as if little has been accomplished. But the day comes when you wake up with a deep feeling inside that the battle has been won! Sure, there's more work to do. Of course, there may be stormy weather ahead. Yes, the harvest is still to come. But you already notice deeper feelings and feel greater intimacy. You become aware of a more genuine respect for yourself and others, and a renewed energy and zest for life. You have a growing confidence in the promise of a full harvest!

A Time to Be Born and a Time to Die . . . A Time to Kill and a Time to Heal

Although Solomon writes about physical life and death, recovery has a parallel cycle of life and death, killing and healing. For the Christian, life truly begins when we ask Christ to become a part of our lives. Yet many of us don't experience the fullness of that new life deep within until we give up control of our lives—until we take our first steps into recovery and realize that we truly need God's help in order to live one day at a time. (See steps one, two, three, and twelve in Appendix A.) To turn away from our old way of living and to seek—through the power of Christ—a new way of living from the heart is to experience new birth.

This new life doesn't come without its share of killing and dying. The monsters that have been held secret in the feelings of our inner child and have hindered our relationships for years must continue to be faced. The memory of a raging, abusive parent must be confronted and worked through. Shame, which can become like a dragon when it is challenged and breathe a fire of defensiveness that seeks to destroy all who come near, must be slain. The image of a physically or emotionally absent parent must be mourned. Twisted memories of sexual abuse must be approached and made powerless. The dark monsters of fear—not only the fears of the past, but also the fears of the present and future—that hold us powerless in their mighty grip, must be exposed in the light of truth. We must also face depression, the seemingly endless well of emotion into which we must plunge deeply in order to draw out the memories that thirst for healing.

Yet even in the midst of the killing, even in the face of death, the healing comes! As we have seen through the examples of those who dared to reach out to the hurting child within, who dared to share their hurt with another human being, who dared to trust God to be with them in the valley of death, *healing will come*. By doing battle with old angers, hurts, and resentments, we will heal.

As we continue to fight the battles, healing will continue to touch every part of our lives. It will touch the old wounds we have suffered in marriage, leading to a wholeness and intimacy that before was unknown. It will provide our children with a model of openness and healing, giving them the opportunity to grow up with less dysfunction and shame in their lives. It will change the way in which we approach our work, enabling us to face the challenges at hand without the weight of unrelated emotional burdens. It will touch relationships in our family of origin, enabling us to set protective boundaries that have never existed or to share feelings that previously have remained unspoken. It will add a new dimension of feeling to our relationship with God.

A Time to Tear Down and a Time to Build . . . A Time to Tear and a Time to Mend

Maintaining growth through the recovery process involves much tearing down and building up. As we grow, we continue to discover old issues, barriers, and patterns that need to be torn down. Out of the rubble, we build new ways of living. For many of us, this means building new boundaries that keep us safe, keep us healthy, and enable the image of God within us to develop its full potential.

It isn't easy to tear apart the way we've always done things or the way we've always thought about things, but it is necessary. Martha and Jim, for instance, were ready to tear down their marriage. Their defensiveness and anger with each other was of atomic proportions. Unfortunately, Martha and Jim were ready to tear down the wrong thing. They didn't need to divorce each other; they each needed to divorce the pain connected with their families of origin!

Martha and Jim both had a great deal of recovery work to do. Martha had been abused by her father for even the most minor mistakes, so whenever Jim brought up an issue, she reacted with anger and defensiveness. As a child, Jim had to tiptoe around his mother, constantly in fear that she would become angry. As they worked through these issues, Martha learned to see that Jim wasn't the same as her father, and Jim learned to see that Martha wasn't the same as his mother. They were able to set boundaries with their parents and appropriately direct their anger back to their parents rather than toward each other. Together they created an emotionally safe relationship that provided the foundation for rebuilding their marriage.

For many of us, recovery involves tearing down and building up in a number of areas. We need to continually set boundaries at work so we don't fall into the trap of compulsive work in order to gain approval from others. We need to set boundaries within our families (immediate as well as extended) so we don't take on responsibilities that belong to others and thereby set the stage for codependency and addiction. We need to set boundaries at church, so we don't commit ourselves to more Christian service than we can handle. These are just a few of the boundaries we must continue to set in order to build up the people God made us to be.

A Time to Weep and a Time to Laugh

The wisdom needed for recovery has been with us for a long time—in the Scriptures. Solomon summarizes it best: Feelings are important. It is good to have a balance of weeping and laughing. When the times of weeping are over, laughter is just around the corner!

When we allow ourselves to feel and to express the depth of our sadness and to rejoice in the fullness of our happy moments, we are set free to feel the full range of our emotions. But when we have been wounded by family dysfunction and shame, we become afraid to feel. We learn to keep a tight lid on our feelings, especially the feelings of hurt. Yet that tight lid destroys the balance of feeling God has created in each of us. It sets up a wall that keeps all of our feelings—not just the forbidden ones—locked deep inside where they are rarely felt. The fullness of our laughter depends, in part, on the depth of our sadness. Thus many of us are limited in our ability to laugh because we have never unlocked the sadness we feel inside.

This was certainly true of Jerry, a successful business-man who began his recovery when he was in his fifties. His wife and children were proud of his accomplishments but wished that he weren't so callous toward their hurts and disappointments. Jerry was always pushing himself toward greater accomplishments and resolved his disappointments by trudging through and working harder. Since he had little empathy for his own feelings, it was difficult for him to care for the feelings of his family.

Although no great crisis occurred in Jerry's life, there was obviously room for improvement. He had been in counseling before, but it was primarily insight-oriented. Therefore he had insight into why he had his problems, but seemed unable to make positive changes in his life. So it was a new experience for him to connect with the feelings of his inner child. What a difference that healing connection made!

As we worked through the feelings of his childhood memories, the emotional prison that Jerry had built inside broke open. He felt the fear he had stuffed inside so long ago and cried giant sobs from the depths of his heart. He reached out and comforted his inner child, who had never felt loved before. For the first time in his life, Jerry felt safe to feel loved, to feel the warmth of his wife's embrace and his children's hugs. He finally realized what a special gift of love God had given to him through his wife and children.

This was the beginning of new growth in Jerry's recovery. Weeks later, he told me how good it felt to be able to give his wife more emotional support. He said, "I've always enjoyed hugging my wife, but it feels so much better now!" His wife noticed that Jerry seemed to understand her feelings better, so she felt freer to talk with him about feelings she previously had kept to herself. Jerry also discovered that he wanted to spend more time with his adult children. Even though they no longer lived at home, he'd take them out to lunch—just to talk!

Jerry went through his time to weep. He took the responsibility to change the old messages of shame and learned that he could feel and laugh!

A Time to Mourn and a Time to Dance

One of the more difficult emotions for adults from dysfunctional families to face is grief and the tears that accompany it. In the same way that Tamar was shamed by her family when she mourned her loss, many of us have been shamed by our families or religious community when we have expressed tears of grief. The lesson of such shaming is clear: It isn't okay to weep.

Often, when people in counseling begin to cry about the hurt or abuse they have suffered, they apologize for crying. Yet weeping is a natural response to pain, a way God has given us to express our sadness and grief. When I think of the shame that some of us associate with feelings of grief, I think of Jesus, who had the strength to allow Himself to feel and express His sorrow.

The story I'm thinking of is in John 11, and it concerns the death of Jesus' dear friend Lazarus. Lazarus had two sisters, Martha and Mary (the woman who poured perfume on Jesus' feet and then wiped them with her hair), and all three of them were close friends of Jesus. Four days after Lazarus died, Jesus went to see the sisters and this is what happened:

When Jesus saw her weeping, and the Jews who had come along with her also weeping, he was deeply moved in spirit and troubled. "Where have you laid him?" he asked.

"Come and see, Lord," they replied.

Jesus wept.

Then the Jews said, "See how he loved him!" (John 11:33–36)

Face-to-face with the death of His friend and the grief of Lazarus' sisters, Jesus wept. He felt the pain. He felt the sadness. He responded with tears, and the Jews had no doubt that He loved Lazarus.

During recovery many of us experience grief, times when we deeply feel the pain of our losses and hurts. We mourn the loss of relationships with family members that through death, divorce, or dysfunction were never allowed to develop. We mourn the loss of childhood that was cut short by abuse or the need to assume adult responsibilities. We feel a deep grief for the hurts we have caused others. There is something very healing, for us and those around us, about giving ourselves permission to grieve deeply and weep freely.

After He wept, Jesus raised Lazarus from the dead. What a time of joy! After the grieving comes an opportunity to dance in joy. Just as life has its normal ebb and flow of mourning and dancing, so also recovery has its times of sorrow and joy. Although those of us in recovery grieve the loss of past relationships, we can celebrate the joy of our present relationships. We may grieve the loss of childhood but celebrate, with childlike jubilation, the joy of living today. We may grieve for the pain we have caused others yet rejoice in making amends.

Feelings of grief and joy as we grow out of the old and into the new are a normal part of human experience. It is normal to feel sadness and joy when a child takes his or her first step. It is normal to celebrate an adolescent's passage into adulthood and to feel a sadness for the stage of life that has passed. As we grow through recovery, we become better able to feel the depth of grief and the fullness of joy.

A Time to Embrace and a Time to Refrain

Life has its times to embrace, its times to hold and be held. An embrace communicates so much. It builds bonds of trust. It says, "I care about you." It expresses affection. It communicates a companionship that says, "You are safe with me when you hurt." An embrace shouts, "I love you!"

An embrace also says, "I want to be close to you." But at times during recovery, intimacy—particularly sexual intimacy—is too big a risk. At those times, an embrace is simply out of the question; it is time to refrain.

When an adult who has been sexually or physically abused begins to connect with the little boy or girl within and work through the feelings and memories associated with the abuse, post-traumatic stress disorder is often magnified. Any closeness can be frightening and overwhelming, setting off feelings of panic or rage. Just a look, a touch, or a kiss can trigger unconscious memories, making the person in recovery feel as though he or she is in the presence of the person who caused the hurt.

At such times, there is no way for closeness to occur. Even holding hands can be a risk of gigantic proportions. During these times a couple's wedding vows, spoken in trust before God, grow in importance. The commitment to love each other "for better or worse, in sickness and health, til death do us part" gains new meaning. In time, with sensitivity, patience, and an openness to share and respect feelings, a couple will once again rejoice in a time for embracing!

A Time to Scatter Stones and a Time to Gather Them . . . A Time to Search and a Time to Give Up . . . A Time to Keep and a Time to Throw Away

Recovery involves dealing with new feelings, redefining one's identity, discovering new ways to relate to people, and changing the rules we live by. That is a tremendous amount of change! It puts a strain on us and our relationships. Although we grow through recovery at whatever pace works best for us, the changes we make through recovery are stressful.

Sometimes we don't know where we are in the recovery process. We don't know whether we're scattering stones or gathering them. We may be searching like crazy, but feel that perhaps we should give up. We may not know what to keep and what to throw away. When we continue our recovery with adequate support (sobriety, a twelve-step group, and therapy), much of the confusion is dispelled. But we have another tool to help us feel and work through our recovery, and that is journaling.

A journal is a private tool for recovery. It is a place where we can write down our hurts, vent our frustrations, explore our feelings, discover our dreams, and record our special thoughts. A journal can help us get through the rough spots in our recovery.

One common rough spot during recovery is communication with God. We can use a journal to share our thoughts with God, which is a form of prayer. We don't have to be afraid to reveal even our darkest thoughts to God. A look at Psalms reveals David's honest dialogue with God. It records his moments of closeness with God and his times of distance; it records his intense anger and his joy. One of the results of recovery is a more intimate relationship with God, and a journal can help build this relationship.

Through a journal, we can get to know our feelings better. We can write down what made us happy and what made us sad. We can record what made us feel good and what made us feel pain. We can fearlessly express feelings about our family, our accomplishments, our failures, our friendships, our work, and our dreams. By doing so, we will clarify the confusion.

Another way we can use a journal is to help our adult self communicate with that little girl or boy within. We can write a dialogue—on any subject, feeling, or issue we choose—between our adult self and our inner child. This will strengthen our identity and relationship with our inner child. By committing our thoughts and feelings to paper through a journal, we gain a better idea of what to scatter or gather, when to search, and what to throw away.

A Time to Be Silent and a Time to Speak

As we grow through recovery incredible feelings are stirred up inside. The ways we communicate to others and how they communicate to us become very important. We need to learn how to communicate what we think and feel, because in doing so we check out the reality of what is rattling around in our heads. Others need to listen to and respect the feelings and needs expressed by the person in recovery, because those feelings are easily shut down again if they are received with rejection. Sometimes this communication is best done through silence; other times, by speaking.

Sometimes silence is the most eloquent support. There is something very special about a person who can stand beside us when we struggle and not need to be heard. I'm not talking about a person who is so codependent that he or she can't share personal issues, but a person who offers deep, healing support simply by being present in a fellow traveler's struggles.

Of course there are times to speak—even times to shout out against evil. There are times when we must care enough to risk confronting the ones we love. Silence, for example, is not appropriate when a child is being shamed or treated unjustly. It would be wrong to be silent when someone close to us is ready to take destructive steps, such as considering an abortion, walking into an affair, or developing an addiction. So recovery involves both silence and speaking, each in its own time.

A Time to Love and a Time to Hate . . .
A Time for War and a Time for Peace

Part of our growth in recovery is an increased ability to experience the full range of emotions that are normal responses to the sometimes insane circumstances of life. At times it is appropriate to love, at times to be frustrated, at times to be sad, at times to be angry, and, yes, at times to hate. As we take responsibility for our recovery, we feel those emotions more intensely, we become better able to express our emotions, and we are more willing to direct our emotions where they belong.

This can be disturbing for others around us. We may be accused of being selfish or self-centered (and may actually feel that way ourselves). We may be told that our expression of emotion is wrong and that we need to forgive and love those who have hurt us. But it is destructive to short-circuit the recovery process by pressing for premature forgiveness. Forgiveness is certainly one of the goals of recovery; yet it cannot occur until we work through our sadness, anger, grief, and whatever other feelings we have buried inside. In fact, forgiveness doesn't happen on our timetable; it happens when it is ready to happen, when the work of recovery is done.

Fortunately, love and peace come after the war! We first have to fight through the battles in order to destroy the dysfunction and shame. But then we are free to let go and forgive. Then we can truly love as we ought. Then we can rejoice in peace.

The beauty of the right timing for love is that when we have worked through our recovery enough to love again, we are able to give love without strings attached. We are able to love when it is needed, not when we need to give it. We are able to love and care freely without the expectation of a response that makes us feel good about ourselves. We are able to understand and love when those we love are hurting too much to give love in return. We are able to love in a way that is like the love of our Savior, Jesus Christ.

Chapter 16

Jesus: Our Model
For Healthy Christian Living

Scripture presents Jesus as the foundation stone of the Church. He is the person around whom everything we believe revolves. He is our salvation. He is the one who brought healing—a healing that can touch us even in the depths of our souls—from heaven down to earth.

Jesus not only brought this healing to earth; He lived it as well. He lived a life of intimate relationships, with Himself, with God, and with those around Him. Out of the wholeness of those relationships, He lived a life of incredible balance—a balance that touched the lives of His disciples so deeply that they spent the rest of their lives spreading His story—and did such a good job that His message of healing is still communicated today!

Yet, like ours, His life wasn't easy. Jesus, too, had to deal with the pain of growing up in a less-than-perfect family. He, too, faced shame. He, too, had to conquer the temptations of codependence and compulsion. Even so, He lived as the ultimate model of healthy Christian living—a model for recovery.

Recovery really is taking the message of Christ and applying it at a relational level. His message isn't just for our intellectual benefit; it touches us deep inside and enables us to heal from the hurts of life. His model of balanced living can touch our hearts today, just as it touched the hearts of His disciples two thousand years ago. When Jesus touches us at a feeling level, it literally changes our lives!

Relationships That Touch the Heart

Recovery is about making changes that bring healing to our lives and relationships. Recovery not only improves the quality of our lives emotionally and spiritually but can make a difference physically as well. Consider this: The medical community has known for some time that relationships have an impact on health and longevity. Recent medical findings continue to validate the healing power of relationships. I have highlighted the results of a few such studies:

> In the Alameda County Study (6,928 men and women living near San Francisco) and in the North Karelia Study (13,301 men and women living in Eastern Finland) participants were studied for five to nine years. Those who were socially isolated had a two- to threefold increased risk of death from both heart disease and all other causes when compared to those who felt most connected to others. These results were independent of other cardiac risk factors, such as cholesterol level, blood pressure, genetics, and so on. Similar results were found in 2,059 subjects from Evans County, Georgia, where the greatest mortality was found in older people with few social ties. . . .

> At Yale University School of Medicine, scientists studied 119 men and 40 women who were undergoing coronary angiography. They found that the more people felt loved and supported, the less coronary atherosclerosis they had at angiography—independent of other risk factors such as age, sex, income, hypertension, serum cholesterol, smoking, diabetes, genetics, and hostility. . . .

> In one study, reported by Dr. William Ruberman in the *New England Journal of Medicine,* interviews with 2,320

male survivors of heart attacks revealed that patients who were classified as being socially isolated and having a high degree of life stress had more than four times the risk of death from heart disease and all other causes when compared with men who had low levels of both stress and isolation. . . .

A report published in the journal *Science* reviewed the mounting evidence that social isolation heightens people's susceptibility to illness. According to Dr. James House, one of the authors of the article, "It's the 10 to 20 percent of people who say they have nobody with whom to share their private feelings, or who have close contact with others less than once a week, who are the most risk."

The report said that "social isolation is as significant to mortality rates as smoking, high blood pressure, high cholesterol, obesity, and lack of physical exercise. In fact, when age is adjusted for, social isolation is as great or greater a mortality risk than smoking. After controlling for the effects of physical health, socioeconomic status, smoking, alcohol, exercise, obesity, race, life satisfaction, and health care, the studies found that those with few or weak social ties were twice as likely to die as those with strong ties." The authors concluded by stating, "Thus, just as we discover the importance of social relationships for health, and see an increasing need for them, their prevalence and availability seem to be declining."[1]

What these studies show is that if you are alone with your feelings—if you keep your hurt, loneliness, anger, and fear deep inside—it will shorten the length and lessen the quality of your life. Conservatively speaking, we can say that a person with dysfunctional relationships is twice as likely to die prematurely than a person with healthy, nurturing relationships. Another way to look at it is to say that trapped feelings can be as damaging to us physically as if we smoked cigarettes. Recovery is, in fact, a matter of life and death!

These studies also point out that although we now realize the physical benefits of supportive, nurturing relationships, it is becoming increasingly difficult for people to have such relationships. This ought not to be true in the Christian community. A supportive relationship should be as close as the person sitting next to us in church. The Christian community—founded on Jesus Christ, the ultimate model of healthy Christian living—has the potential to be one of the most healing forces on earth.

Let's take a look at some highlights of Jesus' life from a relational perspective. Let's see what He faced. Let's see how He dealt with the hard times. Let's see how He handled life and people, how He could be caring and compassionate without being codependent.

Jesus Didn't Have It Easy

Before Jesus even entered the world, His life was shrouded in shame. His mother was pregnant with Him before she got married. It was tough. The shame was overwhelming. When Joseph, her future husband, learned that she was pregnant, he wanted to divorce her. It took a visit from an angel to change his mind! If it had happened in our day, His mother might have wanted an abortion in order to avoid the disgrace.

When He was born, conditions weren't the best. His parents were far away from home, alone in an overcrowded city where they couldn't even find a decent place to sleep—much less to have a baby. So Jesus was born in a manger, surrounded by the smells and sounds of a barn. It wasn't exactly a comfortable, supportive atmosphere for the new parents and baby.

Life didn't get any easier for the new family. Mary and Joseph soon faced the highest stress possible, that of protecting the life of their newborn son from the death orders of King Herod. Fortunately, Joseph paid attention to his dreams, and when an angel told him to take Jesus to Egypt, the family fled.

Can you imagine the fear, anxiety, shame, and tension that Joseph and Mary felt as newlywed parents? Can you imagine what it felt like to be an infant caught in the midst of those feelings? Babies are very much in tune with family emotions. They feel what's happening in the family, so the baby Jesus felt those emotions too. He knew trauma, fear, and shame from His earliest moments of life.

Jesus Had to Set Boundaries with His Family

Scripture doesn't tell us very much about Jesus and His family. We know quite a bit about His birth, but most of our knowledge about His family relationships comes from only three incidents in His life. We'll look at two of those events.

The first took place when Jesus was twelve years old. His family had been in Jerusalem for the Feast of the Passover, and Jesus was accidentally left behind when they headed back to Nazareth (see Luke 2:41–52). His parents looked for Him for three days and finally found Him in the temple. When she saw Jesus, His mother said, "Son, why have you treated us like this? Your father and I have been anxiously searching for you." Sadly, even His mother and stepfather, who had been told by angels that Jesus was the Son of God—the Messiah—didn't understand what that meant in His life.

Jesus' response, however, was direct and to the point. He didn't fall into the emotional trap of saying, "Mom, I'm sorry I treated you badly," for that wasn't the case at all. The fact was that although Jesus was Mary's son, He was also the Son of God. As such, He was responsible to God to do what His heavenly Father would have Him do. So in His response, "Why were you searching for me? Didn't you know I had to be in my Father's house?" Jesus set a boundary with His mother. He made it clear that this was not an emotional issue. The real issue was that Jesus was responsible to God to fulfill God's agenda on earth and that doing so would take Him in a different direction from the rest of the family. Furthermore, His mother's emotional response to that issue was her responsibility, not His.

After making His purpose and priority clear, Jesus returned to Nazareth with His family, "and was obedient to them. . . . And Jesus grew in wisdom and stature, and in favor with God and men" (Luke 2:51–52). So Jesus set the necessary boundaries and continued to grow in relationship with His family, with God, and with other people. That's all we know about Jesus and His family for the next eighteen to twenty years.

The next family interaction we read about took place when Jesus was in His early thirties, in the midst of His ministry on earth. Jesus was preaching to a large crowd, and His mother and brothers came to take Him home (see Mark 3:31–35). They wanted to take Him home because they thought He was out of His mind. They came to rescue Him, to take care of Him.

Once again, just as when Jesus was in the temple in Jerusalem at age twelve, His family did not understand Him. They made decisions about Him and for Him, which shows that they didn't have a clue as to who He was or what He was about. Once again, Jesus let them know that doing His Father's will was of paramount importance to Him. Once again, Jesus set the boundaries that in effect said, "I am fulfilling the responsibilities that God has given to Me. No matter how much I love you and want you to be happy, no matter how upset you may become because I'm not meeting your expectations, I can't let your feelings dictate what I do."

Jesus Set Boundaries Against Evil

Jesus, as the Son of God, not only had to take the risk of setting boundaries with His family but also had to set boundaries against evil—against the devil himself. When the Spirit of God led Jesus into the wilderness to fast for forty days and then to be tested, you'd better believe it was a powerful test (see Matt. 4:1–11)! Jesus was hungry, and the devil tempted Him with food. Jesus was the Son of God, and the devil tempted Him with power, riches, and honor befitting a king. Yet Jesus, who responded with the power of God's Word, set an indisputable boundary against evil.

I think it's interesting that Jesus didn't attempt to set this boundary on His own but did it with the unshakable support of God's Word. After the battle, Jesus wasn't left alone. God sent angels to minister to Him! To me, this is a beautiful image of what support is all about. Jesus took action on the basis of the unfailing support of God's Word and afterward experienced the healing support of God's angels. Those of us who are in recovery need similar support to set the boundaries against evil in our lives. After we have set those difficult boundaries, it is a wonderful blessing to be ministered to by those who support us.

Another time, Jesus had to set a boundary against evil in God's temple (see Matt. 21:12–16). This time, He was not setting a personal boundary but one to protect God's ministry on earth. The temple was being used wrongly, and Jesus, in effect, said, "No! This cannot be done in God's name, in God's house!" He physically drove out everyone who was turning God's temple into a "den of robbers."

After that boundary was set, there was healing! The blind and the lame were healed, and the children in the temple sang His praises! Notice that it was the children who sang His praises, not the adults. In fact, the most powerful adults—the chief priests and the teachers—were angry. That's often the way it is when we set boundaries: Some will be angry with us, but healing will come!

Jesus Maintained His Personal Boundaries

Jesus, the Son of God, needed time for Himself—to meet His personal needs—and wasn't afraid to take it. He didn't seek time alone in order to avoid issues or problems but to commune with His heavenly Father. He knew that an intimate relationship with God the Father was His lifeblood.

It wasn't easy for Jesus to find time alone. No matter where He went or what He needed, the crowds were never far behind. When Jesus was told that John the Baptist had been beheaded, Matthew 14:13 tells us, "he withdrew by boat privately to a solitary place." But when He landed, a huge crowd was waiting for Him. Jesus had compassion on the people and healed them and fed them (see Matt. 14:14–21). Finally, in the evening, He sent the crowd and His disciples away and retreated to the hills to pray (see vv. 22–24).

After His time of prayer, Jesus walked across the water to "catch up" with His disciples, who were crossing the Sea of Galilee by boat. Jesus' walk across the water intrigues me. To me it suggests that Jesus was keenly aware that He had only a limited time on earth, that He could do only so much. Yet He didn't spend every waking moment healing as many people as possible. He didn't live as a compulsive co-dependent who frantically had to make every second count. Instead, He took time out to be alone. He took time out to rest. He took time out to talk with God. And He took time out to walk across the water.

In every area of life, Jesus was perfectly balanced. He identified His responsibilities with incredible clarity and fulfilled them with amazing discipline. Although Jesus did everything with love and compassion, He didn't attempt to do everything. He never assumed responsibility that belonged to another, nor did He allow others to thrust their responsibilities on Him. One example of this perfect balance is His interaction with Peter when He walked out to His disciples' boat on the stormy Sea of Galilee (see Matt. 14:25–33).

When Peter knew it was Jesus who approached them, he jumped out of the boat to meet Him. As Peter walked toward Jesus, he suddenly became afraid, lost his connection with Jesus, and began to sink into the water. If Jesus had been a codependent, He never would have let Peter step out of the boat or begin to sink. A codependent Jesus would have nursed Peter along, making sure the whole adventure went easily. Peter, then, never would have felt his fear, never would have realized his need, and never would have cried out, "Lord, save me!" When Peter screamed for help, Jesus immediately reached out to him. Jesus saved Peter from danger, but He did not rescue him from the doubt, fear, and feelings he needed to face.

Jesus Sets Boundaries to Protect Children

No matter how old we are or how old we become, we are always precious children in God's eyes. God loves us dearly and cares for us deeply. He made that love real to us through the life of His son, Jesus, who came to earth to live, die, and live again so that we might be healed and truly feel His presence in our lives. I think it is very important for us to realize the depth of God's love for children—the depth of His love for the wounded inner child that lives in each of us.

While Jesus was alive on earth, He clearly communicated God's unconditional love for children.

And whoever welcomes a little child like this in my name welcomes me. But if anyone causes one of these little ones who believe in me to sin, it would be better for him to have a large millstone hung around his neck and to be drowned in the depths of the sea." (Matt. 18:5–6)

People were bringing little children to Jesus to have him touch them, but the disciples rebuked them. When Jesus saw this, he was indignant. He said to them, "Let the little children come to me, and do not hinder them, for the kingdom of God belongs to such as these." (Mark 10:13–14)

Jesus had strong words for those who did not value or care for children. He became angry when the disciples sent the children away, as if children were less important than adults. He expressed intense anger at anyone who would cause a child to sin or hinder a child's pursuit of God's kingdom. Jesus didn't stop with strong words. He also set boundaries to ensure that the children were protected and that responsibilities were clearly defined and appropriately maintained. He made it clear that it is absolutely wrong to do anything that would hinder or distort a child's image of God! The message was clear; the line was drawn.

Based on these statements, how do you think Jesus would respond to someone who spiritually, emotionally, physically, or sexually abused a child? Don't you think Jesus will understand our hurt if we have been abused? I believe He does. I believe He understands the pain and anger of an injured child, both when that injury occurs and when the adult works through those feelings in recovery.

Jesus Understands Our Feelings

It may be difficult for some of us to believe this truth deep inside, but Jesus thoroughly understands our struggles. He cares about our hurts and our fears and wants to heal that hurting part of us with His love. It doesn't matter if we were severely traumatized as children, if our parents were alcoholics, or if we grew up in a family that simply didn't know how to handle feelings. He loves us. He understands. We don't have to justify our hurts to Him.

Jesus knows what we have been through. He knows what it is like to grow up in a dysfunctional family. He has felt more shame than most of us can imagine. He knows how hard it is to set boundaries. He knows what it means to be misunderstood. Hebrews 4:15–16 expresses His understanding perfectly!

> *For we do not have a high priest who is unable to sympathize with our weaknesses, but we have one who has been tempted in every way, just as we are—yet was without sin. Let us then approach the throne of grace with confidence, so that we may receive mercy and find grace to help us in our time of need.*

This is our Jesus. A Jesus who understands what it means to feel hated. A Jesus who knows what it is like to be beaten. A Jesus who faced, even as an infant, a crowd of people crying out for His death! A Jesus who faced the rage of an entire race that sought to destroy Him because they thought that if they punished Him enough—if He were dead—their lives would be better.

A Jesus who faced the anger of the "authorities" because He set the right boundaries that make life safe—the boundaries that protect the innocent and allow God's work to be done.

A Jesus who was gentle and made little children feel safe and loved.

A Jesus who was compassionate. A Jesus who could touch the soul of the woman at the well—a woman who thought she was untouchable. A Jesus who could heal the lepers (the AIDS patients of the day).

A Jesus who was tested by the devil in the wilderness. A Jesus who knows how hard it is to be alone and needy. A Jesus who knows how tempting it is to take the easy short-cut and medicate the need—whether it be with food, drugs, alcohol, work, praise, sex—rather than face the pain and draw the line—one moment, one temptation at a time.

A Jesus who could feed thousands, yet turn around and reach out a saving hand to one desperate disciple.

Yes, this is our Jesus.

A Jesus who lived in perfect balance in His relationship with God, with Himself, and with others. A Jesus who even today can bring healing to the depths of our hearts. A Jesus to whom we can confidently take our deepest and darkest hurts, knowing that we will receive His mercy and under-standing.

A Jesus who offers the strength to change. A Jesus who offers a grace that is more than sufficient for our recovery and healing. A Jesus who is the foundation of healthy rela-tionships.

A Jesus who becomes more real when we, as people who have been touched by His healing grace, reach out and min-ister to one another—giving and receiving the support we need to continue our journey of healing and recovery.

Yes, this is Jesus, a son of David and the Son of God, who brings the hope of healing to every heart.

APPENDIX A

The Twelve Steps of Alcoholics Anonymous*

1. We admitted we were powerless over alcohol—that our lives had become unmanageable.

2. Came to believe that a Power greater than ourselves could restore us to sanity.

3. Made a decision to turn our will and our lives over to the care of God as we understood Him.

4. Made a searching and fearless moral inventory of ourselves.

5. Admitted to God, to ourselves and to another human being the exact nature of our wrongs.

6. Were entirely ready to have God remove all these defects of character.

7. Humbly asked Him to remove our shortcomings.

8. Made a list of all persons we had harmed, and became willing to make amends to them all.

9. Made direct amends to such people wherever possible, except when to do so would injure them or others.

10. Continued to take personal inventory and when we were wrong promptly admitted it.

11. Sought through prayer and meditation to improve our conscious contact with God, as we understood Him,

praying only for knowledge of His will for us and the power to carry that out.

12. Having had a spiritual awakening as the result of these steps, we tried to carry this message to alcoholics, and to practice these principles in all our affairs.

*The Twelve Steps are reprinted with permission of Alcoholics Anonymous World Services, Inc. Permission to reprint the Twelve Steps does not mean that AA has reviewed or approved the content of this publication, nor that AA agrees with the views expressed herein. AA is a program of recovery from alcoholism. Use of the Twelve Steps in connection with programs and activities which are patterned after AA but which address other problems does not imply otherwise.

APPENDIX B

Types of Treatment

There are myriad treatment options open to a recovering person. It is important to understand those options and to consider them carefully. You will, for instance, want to ask as many questions as possible; if the person representing the treatment program or therapist is unable to answer freely or openly, go to another program. An organization or program that tends toward defensiveness is not likely to assist a good recovery.

The important thing is to be an advocate for your own treatment or the treatment of your family members. Seeking treatment is one of the most important decisions you or another family member will make, so it is vital that you be as informed as possible about the treatment program that you are considering. The following observations and questions will guide you in seeking treatment.

Twelve-step and Christian Support Groups

Twelve-step groups are as near as your telephone book or local newspaper. The last time I was in my hometown in southern Minnesota (population 1,600), four different twelve-step meetings were listed in the town newspaper. Help is available!

For all practical purposes, twelve-step groups are free. A hat is passed to help pay for coffee and the rent for the room. Even if you have no money, help is just a phone call away. Each meeting has its own personality, and you may need to attend several meetings before you find one where you truly feel at home. I usually recommend that a person attend at least ten meetings before making a final decision. (Frequently, the nature of the particular meeting is less of a problem than an individual's denial and effort to find excuses not to attend.)

Many churches are starting support groups for adults from dysfunctional families, incest victims, and recovering alcoholics and addicts. Many of these groups are very helpful, but it is important that each have, at its core, people who are working through their own recovery. Many times, Christians start support groups out of their own codependency rather than a recognition of their need to give and receive support as part of their recovery.

As a result, these groups are not as helpful as they should be. When a group is functioning well, it will be a safe place in which to share and find acceptance—not judgment. Christian support groups that spiritualize issues without being willing to walk people through the deep hurts will not be too helpful. Support groups that are based on deliverance will not be a safe place for people who are struggling. Although God delivers some people from their problems, my experience has normally been that God is with us as we work through the scary, painful issues.

The Christian twelve-step group I encourage people to attend is Overcomers Outreach, which recognizes Jesus as the "higher power." Designed for anybody who would benefit from a twelve-step group (in my view, everyone!), Overcomers Outreach acts as a bridge between the twelve-step community and the church, and has more than 850 groups in 47 states and 6 countries. I also encourage people to attend a traditional twelve-step group as well. Attending only a Christian support group is rarely enough. It may take two, three, or even seven meetings a week, particularly in the beginning, to do the job.

Outpatient Counseling and Medical Treatment

I work with a family physician, Willard Hawkins, M.D., who considers the whole family picture. I do this because there is often an underlying medical condition that needs treatment in addition to the spiritual and psychological problems a person may face. So I suggest that anyone beginning a recovery process get a complete physical too. Your family physician can play an important role in the recovery process, particularly if he or she is supportive of twelve-step work and understands the impact that a dysfunctional family can have on a person's overall health.

Many types of counselors are available to provide treatment. Most therapists have at least a master's degree and frequently have a doctorate in psychology (Psy.D.) or a doctorate of philosophy (Ph.D.). Psychiatrists are trained to prescribe and administer medications for depression, anxiety, psychosis, and other disorders. Some have also received training in psychotherapeutic interventions. Licensed clinical social workers (L.C.S.W.) sometimes specialize in psychotherapy. Most individual, marital, and family problems can be handled through a combination of support groups and outpatient psychotherapy. A person should be hospitalized to work through difficult issues only after careful evaluation of the need for hospitalization and the type of hospital program required.

Do not assume that people in any of the above specialties are knowledgeable about dysfunctional family issues, codependency, addictive diseases, or inner child work. Ask many questions concerning training, experience, and knowledge of the need for twelve-step and other support groups. Also keep in mind that psychotherapy is not, in itself, enough. A person in recovery needs to regularly attend a support group that meets his or her need. It is helpful if that person can also attend a church that is supportive of recovery.

As you begin to narrow down the treatment options, ask questions about cost, length, and frequency of the sessions. If you have insurance, it may cover none, some, or all of the costs of outpatient psychotherapy. With the shift to managed health care where more and more services are provided through preferred provider organizations (PPOs) or health maintenance organizations (HMOs), the reimbursement for outpatient services is often limited, as is the number of sessions that is covered. As insurance companies cut back on their benefits, more and more of the cost of treatment is left in the hands of the consumer.

Inpatient Treatment

There are several factors to consider when taking the step toward inpatient hospitalization. If the family member is expressing suicidal thoughts and intent, for instance, it is better not to take chances but to move toward immediate hospitalization. Once hospitalization occurs, the psychotherapist and psychiatrist will work together to assess the degree of inpatient treatment that will be required.

If the family member suffers from alcoholism, a drug addiction, an eating disorder, or a sexual addiction, a period of inpatient treatment will probably be needed. With addictive disease, there is usually a period of detoxification that should be medically supervised. Withdrawal without such supervision can be dangerous—in some cases leading to heart attacks and strokes. In the hospital, staff members can help stabilize the person physically so that he or she can begin to take responsibility for doing what is needed to maintain sobriety.

Hospitalization may also be required when the patient's history reveals chronic sexual, physical, or emotional abuse. In the early stages of recovery, painful memories and feelings may return with such intensity that the person cannot handle them on an outpatient basis. The person then cannot function normally and will need the daily, intensive work on past memories and the constant support that is available only in a hospital setting.

As you check out hospital options, do not assume that all Christian programs or traditional hospital programs are twelve-step oriented. Most hospital programs market their services for treating alcoholism, eating disorders, sexual addiction, codependency, and other disorders but do not ground their patients in twelve-step work. Even Christian programs do not always provide the basics of sound treatment for these disorders. Any person will appear to do better in the hospital because the day is structured with adequate rest, regular meals, and exercise, and there are enough people to provide support and a safe place in which to share feelings. Yet when a person leaves the hospital without being grounded in twelve-step work, he or she is set up for failure.

Before making a decision, it is crucial to consider the costs of hospitalization. As with outpatient treatment, the rise of managed health care has limited the money available for inpatient treatment. It is best to get a written statement of how much your insurance company will pay toward treatment. It is also important to get in writing the hospital's anticipated costs. If someone on the hospital staff says that they will accept what your insurance will pay as full payment, do not rely on that statement unless you have a written commitment. I have seen situations where the insurance company approved inpatient treatment but later refused to pay, leaving the patient with an enormous bill.

Day Treatment and Partial Hospitalization

Day treatment or partial hospitalization programs are becoming more popular due to the high cost of inpatient treatment. Day treatment means that the patient and his or her family attend the hospital program during the day and stay at a nearby hotel or their own home at night. This can reduce the cost of treatment considerably without affecting the benefits of intensive daily treatment.

Recovery Homes and Halfway Houses

These programs are often operated in large homes and are beginning to meet the need for residential care without the high cost of a hospital program. These facilities provide a wide range of treatment—from the same treatment the patient would receive in an inpatient program to primarily custodial care. Again, it is important to inquire about the quality of the program, the experience of the staff, and the percentage of the cost that will be covered by insurance.

APPENDIX C

Helpful Organizations

Overcomers Outreach, Inc.
2290 West Whittier Boulevard, Suite A/D
La Habra, CA 90631
(213) 697-3994

Overcomers Outreach, Inc., is a nonprofit, Christ-centered ministry dedicated to helping anyone who would benefit from a twelve-step program. The organization also helps churches establish Christ-centered twelve-step support groups. As of this writing, there are more than 900 Overcomers Outreach groups in 47 states and 6 countries. Internationally, Overcomers Outreach, Inc. is supported by the tax-deductible contributions of individuals who believe in its goals or have benefited from the program.

Overcomers Outreach is not intended to replace such twelve-step groups as A.A., Al-Anon, or A.C.O.A. Rather, the organization seeks to supplement those programs and assist Christians who are in recovery. Overcomers Outreach views itself as a bridge between the twelve-step community and churches of all denominations. Its founders are Bob and Pauline Bartosh, who started the ministry based on their own recovery experience.

If you are interested in starting a Christian twelve-step support group in your church, contact Overcomers Outreach by phone or mail. Ask for *Freed*, a booklet available in English or Spanish that contains all the information you'll need to conduct an Overcomers Outreach group. If an Overcomers Outreach group does begin in your area, please inform the central office so that people who call for information can be referred to your group. Overcomers Outreach also has additional materials on recovery and starting recovery groups, which is available from the central office.

Other Twelve-Step Support Groups

Adult Children of Alcoholics
Central Service Board
P.O. Box 35623
Los Angeles, CA 90035
(213) 464-4423

Alcoholics Anonymous
P.O. Box 459
Grand Central Station
New York, NY 10163
(212) 686-1100

Al-Anon/Alateen Family
Group Headquarters
P.O. Box 182
Madison Square Station
New York, NY 10159
(800) 344-2666
(212) 302-7240

Debtors Anonymous
314 West 53rd Street
New York, NY 10018
(212) 969-0710

Emotions Anonymous
P.O. Box 4245
St. Paul, MN 55104
(612) 647-9712

Gamblers Anonymous
P.O. Box 17173
Los Angeles, CA 90017
(213) 386-8769

Incest Survivors Anonymous
P.O. Box 5613
Long Beach, CA 90800

Narcotics Anonymous
World Service Office
16155 Wyandotte Street
Van Nuys, CA 91406
(818) 780-3951

National Association for
Children of Alcoholics
31582 Coast Highway,
Suite B
South Laguna, CA 92677
(714) 499-3889

National Clearinghouse for
Alcohol Information
P.O. Box 1908
Rockville, MD 20850

Overeaters Anonymous,
World Service Office
2190 190th Street
Torrance, CA 90504
(213) 542-8363

Victims of Incest
Recover Through
Understanding, Education
and Support (VIRTUES)
P.O. Box 602
Brea, CA 92622-0602

Sinners Anonymous
P.O. Box 26001
Austin, TX 78755-0001

APPENDIX D

Suggested Reading

Alcoholics Anonymous: The Story of How Many Thousands of Men and Women Have Recovered from Alcoholism. New York: Alcoholics Anonymous World Services, Inc., 1976.

Bradshaw, John. *The Family: A Revolutionary Way of Self-Discovery*. Deerfield Beach, FL: Health Communications, 1988.

_____. *Healing the Shame That Binds You*. Deerfield Beach, FL: Health Communications, 1988.

Buhler, Rich. *Pain and Pretending: You Can Be Set Free from the Hurts of the Past*. Nashville: Thomas Nelson, 1988.

Carder, Dave, Earl Henslin, Henry Cloud, John Townsend, and Alice Brawand. *Secrets of Your Family Tree: Healing for Adult Children of Dysfunctional Families*. Chicago: Moody Press, 1991.

Cloud, Henry. *When Your World Makes No Sense: Four Critical Decisions That Can Bring Hope and Direction into Your Life*. Nashville: Oliver-Nelson, 1988.

Dr. Bob and the Good Oldtimers: A Biography with Recollections of Early A.A. in the Midwest. New York: Alcoholics Anonymous World Services, Inc., 1980.

Feldmeth, Joann, and Midge Finley. *We Weep for Ourselves and Our Children*. San Francisco: Harper & Row, 1990.

Fossum, M., and M. Mason. *Facing Shame*. New York: Norton, 1986.

Kaufman, Gershen. *The Psychology of Shame: Theory and Treatment of Shame-Based Syndromes*. New York: Springer Publishing Co, 1989.

_____. *Shame: The Power of Caring*. Cambridge, MA: Schenkman Books, 1985.

Klimek, David. *Beneath Mate Selection and Marriage: The Unconscious Motives in Human Pairing*. New York: Van Nostrand Reinhold Company, 1979.

May, Gerald. *Addiction and Grace*. San Francisco: Harper & Row, 1988.

McFarland, B., and T. Bauman. *Feeding the Empty Heart*. New York: Harper/Hazelden, 1987.

McFarland, B., T. Bauman, and Tyeis Baker-Baumand. *Shame and Body Image: Culture and the Compulsive Eater*. Deerfield Beach, FL: Health Communications, 1990.

Mellody, Pia, Andrea Wells Miller, and J. Keith Miller. *Facing Codependence: What It Is, Where It Comes from, How It Sabotages Our Lives*. San Francisco: Harper & Row, 1989.

Miller, J. Keith. *A Hunger for Healing: The Twelve Steps as a Classic Model for Christian Spiritual Growth*. San Francisco: Harper & Row, 1991.

Parham, A. Philip. *Letting God: Christian Meditations for Recovering Persons*. San Francisco: Harper & Row, 1987.

Potter-Efron, Ronald, and Patricia Potter-Efron. *Letting Go of Shame: Understanding How Shame Affects Your Life*. Center City, MN: Hazelden, 1989.

Spickard, Anderson, and Barbara Thompson. *Dying for a Drink: What You Should Know About Alcoholism*. Dallas: Word, Inc., 1985.

The Twelve Steps: A Spiritual Journey by Friends in Recovery. San Diego: Recovery Publications, 1988.

VanVonderan, Jeff. *Tired of Measuring Up: Getting Free from the Demands, Expectations, and Intimidations of Well-Meaning People*. Minneapolis: Bethany House Publishers, 1989.

Woititz, Janet. *Adult Children of Alcoholics*. Deerfield Beach, FL: Health Communications, 1983.

NOTES

Chapter 1

1. John F. Walvoord and Roy B. Zuck, *The Bible Knowledge Commentary* (Wheaton: Victor Books, 1986). "The meeting was superficially cordial, but as subsequent events demonstrated, David's long delayed acceptance of his son came too late. Absalom was embittered and resolved to do whatever was necessary to make David pay for his intransigence."

Chapter 3

1. John of Salisbury, *Policraticus* (New York: F. Ungar Publishing Co., 1979).

Chapter 6

1. John Bradshaw, *The Family* (Deerfield Beach, FL: Health Communications, Inc., 1988), 150.
2. Rodney Clapp, "Shame Crucified," *Christianity Today,* March 11, 1991, 27.

Chapter 7

1. M. Fossum and M. Mason, *Facing Shame* (New York: Norton, 1986).
2. Fossum and Mason.

Chapter 13

1. Anne Wilson Schaef, *Laugh! I Thought I'd Die If I Didn't: Daily Meditations of Healing Through Humor* (New York: Ballantine Books, 1990).
2. My view on boundaries is inspired by the work of Salvador Minuchin, *Families and Family Therapy* (Cambridge: Harvard University Press, 1974); and Pia Mellody with J. Keith and Andrea Wells Miller, *Facing Codependence* (San Francisco: Harper & Row, 1989).

Chapter 16

1. "Your Healthy Heart," *Prevention,* February 1991.

ABOUT THE AUTHOR

Earl R. Henslin is a licensed marriage, family, child therapist. His Fullerton, California, practice through Henslin and Associates focuses on marriage, family, child counseling, and he conducts training sessions and seminars for professionals such as pastors, physicians, and therapists who work in these areas. He holds the doctor of clinical psychology degree from Rosemead Graduate School of Biola University, where he is a part-time instructor. He is a member of the California Association of Marriage and Family Therapists and the Christian Association of Psychological Studies.

A nationally acclaimed speaker on issues related to Christians and recovery, Dr. Henslin is also Chairman of the Board of Overcomers Outreach, a nonprofit ministry that assists local churches in establishing twelve-step support groups dealing with recovery from codependency, sexual trauma, addictions, eating and panic disorders, depression, and problems related to dysfunctional families.

He lives in La Habra, California, with his wife, Karen, and their four children, Ben, Rachel, Amy, and Jill.

Henslin and Associates provides outpatient treatment and networks with different inpatient treatment facilities for the treatment of adults concerned with codependency, incest, alcoholism, drug addiction, eating disorders, sexual addiction, men's issues, and other issues of dysfunctional families. Dr. Henslin conducts seminars on these issues for churches, Christian organizations, counseling centers, and businesses. For information concerning treatment programs or seminars, please contact:

Earl R. Henslin, Psy.D., M.F.C.C.
2720 North Harbor Boulevard, Suite 200
Fullerton, California 92635